Waterfalls

Waterfalls

The Niagara Escarpment

Jerry Lawton

Photographs by Mikal Lawton

The BOSTON
MILLS PRESS

To my mother, Dorothy, who cheered us on

CATALOGUING IN PUBLICATION DATA

Lawton, Jerry, 1935–
Waterfalls: the Niagara Escarpment

ISBN 1-55046-313-6

1. Waterfalls — Ontario — Niagara Escarpment
— Guidebooks. 2. Niagara Escarpment (Ont.)
Guidebooks. 3. Trails — Ontario — Niagara
Escarpment — Guidebooks.
I. Lawton, Mikal, 1970– . II. Title.

GB1430.N52L38 2000   917.1304'4
00-930658-7   *917.1339*
LAW

Copyright ©2000 Jerry Lawton and Mikal Lawton

Published in 2000 by
BOSTON MILLS PRESS
132 Main Street
Erin, Ontario N0B 1T0
Tel 519-833-2407
Fax 519-833-2195
e-mail books@bostonmillspress.com
www.bostonmillspress.com

An affiliate of
STODDART PUBLISHING CO. LIMITED
34 Lesmill Road
Toronto, Ontario, Canada
M3B 2T6
Tel 416-445-3333
Fax 416-445-5967
e-mail gdsinc@genpub.com

Distributed in Canada by
GENERAL DISTRIBUTION SERVICES LIMITED
325 Humber College Boulevard
Toronto, Canada M9W 7C3
Orders 1-800-387-0141 Ontario & Quebec
Orders 1-800-387-0172 NW Ontario
& other provinces
e-mail cservice@genpub.com

Distributed in the United States by
GENERAL DISTRIBUTION SERVICES INC.
PMB 128, 4500 Witmer Industrial Estates,
Niagara Falls, New York 14305-1386
Toll-free 1-800-805-1083
Toll-free fax 1-800-481-6207
e-mail gdsinc@genpub.com
www.genpub.com

Cover design by Gillian Stead and Mary Firth
Design by Mary Firth
Map drawings by Mikal Lawton and Mary Firth
Printed in Canada

Front cover photo: Twin waterfalls in the
village of Walter's Falls.
Title page photo: DeCew Falls.

THE CANADA COUNCIL | LE CONSEIL DES ARTS
FOR THE ARTS | DU CANADA
SINCE 1957 | DEPUIS 1957

We acknowledge for their financial support of our
publishing program the Canada Council, the
Ontario Arts Council, and the Government of Canada
through the Book Publishing Industry
Development Program (BPIDP).

Contents

Acknowledgments   6

Introduction   7

Niagara Falls   12
DeCew Falls   20
Swayze Falls   28
Rockway Falls   31
Louth Falls   33
Balls Falls   36
Thirty Mile Creek Falls   40
Beamer's Falls   43
The Devil's Punch Bowl   45
Felker's Falls   49
Albion Falls   51
Buttermilk Falls   53
Chedoke Falls   54
Tiffany Falls   57
Mill Falls   59
Sherman Falls   64
Hermitage Falls   66

Heritage Falls   68
Webster's Falls   70
Tews Falls   75
Borer's Falls   79
Grindstone Falls   82
Hilton Falls   85
The Cataract   89
Hogg's Falls   93
Eugenia Falls   95
Lavender Falls   100
Anthea's Falls   101
Walter's Falls   104
Inglis Falls   108
Jones Falls   112
Indian Falls   115

The Escarpment
   Hither and Yon   118

Photographing Waterfalls   123

Acknowledgments

We owe our deepest gratitude to Elsa Franklin for being our champion, to Sue Powell of the Niagara Escarpment Commission for her cheerful attempts to steer us right, to Henrik Thalenhorst of Strathcona Mineral Services for his patient efforts to keep us from saying foolish things about geology, to John James for introducing us to the wonders of GPS satellite tracking devices, to John Denison, Noel Hudson, Kathy Fraser and Mary Firth of Boston Mills Press for taking us through the process of publication with care and good humor, and to Tom East for sharing his personal story with us. We also want to thank Gary Konkle and Greg Miller of the Friends of the Morningstar Mill, the late Linda Smith of the St. Catharines Department of Recreation and Community Services, Kim Frolich of the Niagara Peninsula Conservation Authority, Scott Peck of the Hamilton Region Conservation Authority, Jane Hyslop of the County of Grey-Owen Sound Museum, Nancy White of the Grey Sauble Conservation Foundation, Donna Russell of the South Grey Museum, John Riley of the Nature Conservancy of Canada, Bill Swenor of the Michigan Geological Survey, Bob Reszka and Milt Gere of the Michigan Department of Natural Resources, and Dr. Don Mikulic of the Illinois Geological Survey.

> By night and day, in sunshine or in storm, water is always the most sublime feature in a landscape, and no view can be truly grand in which it is wanting.
>
> Susanna Moodie (1803–1885)

MAPS LEGEND

406	Provincial highway	+++++ Rail line	
312	County road		Escarpment
- - - -	Bruce Trail		
o	Waterfall location		Bridge

Introduction

Hamilton is a far from inviting city when you see it from the Burlington Skyway. From that perspective, with the steel mills imposing themselves on its skyline, what one sees is what many believe the city to be — the ultimate symbol of smoky progress. In a diabolical way, that may be just what some Hamiltonians want strangers to think; it keeps Torontonians from discovering and over-running the city's hidden treasures.

It's hard to imagine that just beyond the gray, forbidding waters of Burlington Bay there's something as lovely as Cootes Paradise, that exquisite body of water that is the centerpiece of the vast forested lands of the Royal Botanical Gardens. Or that just beyond that is the inestimable Dundas Valley, a broad riverless tract of forest and meadow that lies between the pretty town of Dundas on the one side and the even prettier town of Ancaster on the other. Here, Hamiltonians and their neighbors have the pleasures of some of the best hiking, biking and cross-country ski trails in Canada.

It's even harder to imagine that on the horseshoe-shaped section of the Niagara Escarpment that rims the city there are 15 waterfalls — you can count 'em — 15 of them! And most are more than fanciful trickles. The majority are as high as a three- or four-story building or higher. One's almost as high as Niagara! And they're all different. No two are even vaguely alike. Some are tall, wispy ribbon falls. Others are broad curtains of thundering whitewater. Still others are long, splashy runs of linking cascades. How many people, even in Hamilton, have any idea that there are this many waterfalls within or just beyond the city's boundaries? And how many have visited them all or even know where to find them?

Hamilton was my home when I was a little boy. I can remember hiking with my Wolf Cub pack along the banks of Red Hill Creek, remember how we trekked through King's Forest — a city park as magnificent as it sounds — and how we struggled up a deep, dark gorge to Buttermilk Falls. I can recall standing there and looking up into the sky in awe, watching the long ribbons of water fall toward me and splash in the shiny pool at my feet. It was the first waterfall I had ever seen, and I was enthralled.

I would be more than half a century further along in life before I would discover, to my astonishment, that there is another waterfall that is even more spectacular and far lovelier just minutes away from Buttermilk — Albion Falls.

Much before that, it was my good luck to discover Webster's Falls. I was drawn to it by an article in a Toronto newspaper, an article I don't believe anyone else read, because there was nobody there when I found this unexpected bit of paradise perched on the edge of the Escarpment above Dundas. Ever since then, this miniature version of Niagara has remained for me one of the most tranquil, out-of-this-world places I know. The little park that graces the crest of the falls, with its weathered stone bridge and stone picnic pavilions, its mammoth willows and cedars and oaks, looks like something that has come to us untouched, right out of the 1920s and 1930s. It has an enchanting air to it that curiously reminds me of Frances Hodgson Burnett's *The Secret Garden*.

My wife and I visited Webster's before we were married. We picnicked there with our son, Mikal, when he was a little boy. When he was grown up and studying photographic arts at university, we went there looking for pictures to take. Only then, 25 years later, did we discover that Webster's has a companion waterfall, Tews Falls, just minutes away on foot. It's equally lovely but startlingly different in character.

That made us stop and think: if it was that easy for us to overlook a feature as substantial and accessible as Tews Falls, how many other waterfalls had we missed? In the long stretch of the Escarpment, from Niagara to Tobermory, just how many waterfalls were there, anyway?

We searched for books on the subject and found none. The maps we consulted, when they did indicate the presence of a waterfall, were sometimes confused about its location. Only one map, for example, a standard highway map, had the elusive Chedoke Falls marked, but it was shown to be a kilometer or two away from where we actually found it.

It was the meticulous *Bruce Trail Guide* that convinced us that there were surely dozens of waterfalls in the 725 kilometers' (450 miles) length of the Niagara Escarpment. We decided to go looking for them, first because Mikal wanted new subject matter for his camera, then because the hunt proved so satisfying we decided to do a book about them.

We came to think of it as "collecting" waterfalls. That's how we went about it, and that's how we hope you will too. Each time we came home, tired and happy from our explorations of the resplendent Ontario countryside, we had another two or three falls to add to our list. It was great fun. Over and over we experienced the excitement and anticipation that comes with first hearing a waterfall but not seeing it, then the thrill of spotting it at last, of seeing how different each one is.

By some counts there are as many as 70 waterfalls on the Escarpment. A number of them are rather small. Washboard Falls, which is near Ancaster, is one. It's a pretty little thing, small enough to fit into your backyard — don't we all wish! Many of the smaller falls belong to larger cascades. The magnificent Rockway Falls, just west of St. Catharines, has four or five miniature waterfalls subsidiary to it. We haven't included these smaller ones in our count except for those that have an interesting story attached to them, such as Heritage Falls and Anthea's Falls. In truth, we didn't want to diminish the impact or the excitement of searching for the 30 or so waterfalls that really are of some size.

If Niagara is the great soaring cathedral of waterfalls, then the others are analogous to beautiful little chapels, as peaceful and spirit-lifting as any created by human hands. Because there are so many of them and because they're usually tucked away out of sight, without even a simple sign to acknowledge their existence, you can often have them completely to yourself, especially on a weekday, even in the summer.

High summer isn't, in fact, the best time to visit most waterfalls. The levels in many streams have dropped dramatically and some falls are reduced to a disappointing trickle or dry up completely. Spring is better in every way. There's lots of water. Everything is fresh and green. And in early spring, before the leaves come on the trees, you can take photos from a good many more vantage points. Fall is a good time too. Water levels are back to normal and the autumn colors make everything that much lovelier. The most surprising time of the year is midwinter. Then you have the spectacular buildup of ice around the waterfalls. It's then that you can find yourself witness to a beauty that is almost frightening.

"You're going to get yourself a four-by-four, aren't you?" a friend asked when he heard what we were up to. "You can't do it in the Buick."

Well, we did do it in the Buick, and easily, too. It's true the waterfalls are part of some of the most rugged terrain in Southern Ontario, but in almost every case there's a good road that will take you right to them. In fact, the roads were built because the falls were there.

When the first settlers came to the Niagara Peninsula in the 1780s, the waterfalls were the only source of power that could run the sawmills and gristmills. For the next 80 years, as the lands bordering the Escarpment were slowly opened up all the way to the Bruce Peninsula, the waterfalls became essential to the success of the new settlements. What an irony! What once were centers of industrial development surrounded by vast hinterlands of wilderness are now centers of wilderness surrounded by vast hinterlands of industrial development. This unlikely transformation has happened within the lifetime of many people who are still living. For 150 years, from the end of the American Revolutionary War until just before the Second World War, the waterfalls were an important element of commercial life. It's since then that most of them have reverted to wilderness.

It was suggested that in addition to writing about the waterfalls we also do a rundown of local restaurants, museums, theme parks, and so on. We certainly toyed with the idea, for there is much to do and see along the Escarpment. In the end we decided against it. There's so much to tell about the waterfalls themselves — about their surroundings, their history and the people who discovered them and settled next to them. Suffice it to say that wherever you go, you won't find yourself much more than 15 minutes away from a restaurant. And the tourist information centers and bookstores are full of books, booklets and brochures about local attractions.

You can certainly look upon the waterfalls as destinations, something to aim for when you're headed for a day in the country. And if you find the Bruce Trail a little forbidding and the sturdy breed of hiker who inhabits it a little intimidating, the waterfalls are an easy, gentle means of introduction. There are side trails or loops around many of them. These will provide you with a hike of a kilometer or two, sometimes three or four. They're a perfect way to put yourself and the trail to the test. Are you up to it physically? Is it something you'd like to try on a more serious level? You can certainly take your measure from us. Throughout the book we've chronicled some of our own experiences in the hope that you'll not only be infected by our enthusiasm but also instructed by our physical accomplishments and limitations. A fit person won't find any of it difficult.

If it's a few hours of tranquility you're looking for, you can, as we've said, expect to have many of the waterfalls pretty much to yourself on most days. Or, if you find you simply can't afford to shell out another $150 plus to take the kids to a hockey game or baseball game, you'll find the waterfalls will cost you almost nothing. The Conservation Authorities do charge an entry or a parking fee at three or four locations, but it's definitely less, maybe a lot less, than you'll pay for parking in the vicinity of the SkyDome or the Air Canada Centre.

We've tried to be meticulous with our directions, some of you will say too meticulous. There are shorter ways to get to some of the falls than we've indicated, as you'll no doubt discover after a visit or two. We've tailored our directions for people who are complete strangers to each area and attempted to guide them along routes that are not too complicated to follow. None of the waterfalls, as we've said, is out of the way, but it's easy to miss a turn and get lost.

If you own a handheld satellite positioning device, you can take advantage of the U.S. Defense Department's Global Position System (GPS). The coordinates for each waterfall are listed along with the height and crest width. If you don't own one, maybe you have a sport-fishing relative or neighbor who does. It makes "collecting" waterfalls that much more interesting. You can, of course, use the same coordinates to find the waterfalls on government topographical maps, though it will cost you $100 or more to buy the maps that cover the Escarpment from Niagara to Owen Sound. (North of Owen Sound the streams all flow away from the Escarpment. Because of that there are no waterfalls — or so we presumed. More about that later.)

Buy the *Bruce Trail Guide!* It's not expensive — about what you'd spend for hot dogs and pop when you take the kids to a game. The maps are excellent, more useful in many ways than the government maps, and they snap out so that you can stick them in your pocket. In addition, it'll give you a lot of information about the trail, the Niagara Escarpment, and the things to be found along the way.

In giving the height and width of each falls, we've tried to use figures from sources that are relatively reliable. In some cases we simply couldn't find figures and had to make our own estimates on site. They won't be good enough to satisfy a geologist or an engineer but they will give you a reasonable idea of the size of the thing you're looking for.

By indicating the direction each waterfall faces and whether or not it's under tree cover, we've tried to be helpful to those of you who take photographs. We've also concluded the book with a chapter of tips on photographing waterfalls.

Finally, a word about terminology. We've learned to live with the illogical circumstance that makes the word "falls" singular as well as plural. It's more difficult to stay on the side of the angels when you're trying to make sense of the mess — melange is a better word — that has been made of our attempt to convert from imperial to metric measurement. Only a Canadian would tell you to go two kilometers down the road and then follow the path for 200 feet to get to the waterfall. Throughout we've tried to write it as people use it. If it's a distance of less than 100 meters, it's in feet. If it's over 100, it's in meters or kilometers, and so on.

The day I sat down to write this introduction, I saw in a magazine a sumptuous full-page ad designed to lure me to Costa Rica. The most seductive of several photos was one of a waterfall, a pretty waterfall, yes, but not more lovely or enticing than the waterfalls you'll read about in this book. We have a tendency to think of things close to home as ordinary. With this book, in our own small way, we hope to convince you that there are many things right here in Ontario that are far from ordinary.

Beware!

The Niagara Escarpment is a dangerous place. Anyone who has ever peered into one of its deep gorges or stood in awe of its soaring bluffs knows that already. One of the best spots from which to view spectacular Rockway Falls, for example, is a slab of rock that hangs high above the rapids. There's no wall, no fence, no guardrail to stop you from going over. Your life is entirely in your own hands. It's at least 100 feet straight down to the swirling waters below. If 100 feet doesn't sound very impressive, think of it as the equivalent of an eight- or nine-story building.

Responsible adults don't have to be told to look out for themselves and their loved ones. And irresponsible ones don't pay heed in any case.

The best way to avoid danger, as any old pilot will tell you, is to make yourself aware of when and where danger exists. For example, no parents would let a child wander close to the edge of a gorge but they might not be so protective of the family pet. Animals don't have an instinct for such things. A city-bred dog, all fired up with the excitement of new territory to explore, is in real danger of plunging over the edge as he goes charging through brush and undergrowth without caution.

So raise that little red warning flag somewhere in the back of your mind and keep it flying. It won't get in the way of having a good time. It won't turn out to be the worst day of your life, either.

We repeat: There are few walls, fences or guardrails to hold you back. You have to look out for yourself.

Niagara Falls
On the Niagara River

HORSESHOE FALLS
Height – 54 m (175.5 ft)   Crest Width – 675 m (2,194 ft)   N 43:04:84   W 79:04:80

AMERICAN FALLS
Height – 56 m (182 ft)   Crest Width – 320 m (1040 ft)   N 43:05:14   W 79:04:29

BRIDAL VEIL FALLS
Height – 56 m (182 ft)   Crest Width – 12 m (39 ft)

Best Time to View: Any day of the year. Try a winter visit if you want to see Niagara when it looks spectacularly different. Horseshoe Falls faces north. The American and Bridal Veil Falls face west. All three are curtain falls.

Responsible Authority: Niagara Parks Commission, (905) 356-2241. Niagara Falls State Park, (716) 278-1770.

How to Get There: Everybody, of course, knows how to get to Niagara Falls. But if you're in the habit of taking the QEW all the way, for a change try getting off at Exit 38 and taking the old York Road (Niagara County Road 81) into Queenston. It's one of Ontario's oldest and most historic towns, home of Laura Secord and, for a brief time, William Lyon Mackenzie. From here you can look up at the famous Queenston Heights and the towering monument to General Sir Isaac Brock.

By taking the Niagara Parkway south to the Falls, you can treat yourself to what Winston Churchill once called one of the great Sunday drives in the world. But before you do, look up one more time at that great hill. What you see is not Queenston Heights alone but the Niagara Escarpment. On this very spot, about 12,000 years ago, the world's most famous waterfall came into being.

For a while we considered leaving Niagara out of this guide entirely. We were afraid its inclusion would overwhelm and detract from what we had to say about the other waterfalls of the Escarpment. There were people who urged us to do just that. "It's such a cliché," said one acquaintance. But in the end, we decided it had to be in. This is, after all, a guide to the waterfalls of the Escarpment, and Niagara Falls is indisputably a part of the Niagara Escarpment.

We agonized even more about our ability to find something fresh and intriguing to say about the Falls. What's left after the indefatigable Pierre Berton and 10,000 other writers have been there before you?

As for photos, well, they've been taking pictures of the Falls almost from the moment photography was invented. There isn't a foot of ground that you can physically get to that a million people haven't already stood upon with camera in hand.

A coy November sun breaks through the gloom at Niagara.

What's striking about all this is how assiduously people have gone about try-ing to capture, in words and pictures, the essence of the Falls. And how others have tried to outperform it with acts of daring or showmanship or enterprise. All have failed. You simply can't convey the awesome beauty and greatness of Niagara in mere words and photographs, and you can't upstage it, no matter how courageous, imaginative or outrageous you are.

So we decided that the story to tell was the story of the great waterfall itself.

To begin, it's not the biggest waterfall in the world. It's far from the highest, and it's not quite the largest in volume. At first we were led to believe that a water-fall called Sete Quedas was the biggest. It's in South America, on the Rio Parana, close to where Brazil, Paraguay and Argentina meet. We should say "was" rather than "is," because when we looked it up a second time, in a newer reference book, Sete Quedas had disappeared. It wasn't on any current list of the world's largest waterfalls. It had ceased to have any visible presence because they had drowned it, flooded it out in an enormous hydroelectric development. It's inconceivable that anyone would dare think to do such a thing to Niagara Falls. Altering or abusing it is prohibited by treaty. Canada and the United States are even limited in the amount of water they're allowed to divert to generate electrical power.

The loss of Sete Quedas moved Niagara Falls up the list of the world's biggest waterfalls from third to second. Only Kone Falls in the Mekong Delta in Southeast

Asia is greater in volume. Even without Sete Quedas, the south central part of South America still has the largest concentration of great waterfalls on Earth, with four of the top six, including the magnificent Iguacu, which is really a spectacular grouping of some 270 waterfalls.

If Niagara doesn't quite win it on size, it does on quality. Most of the world's truly big waterfalls run heavy with silt, in unbecoming shades of brown and yellow. Niagara, in contrast, is fed by the clear waters of four of the five Great Lakes, lakes that drain nearly 700,000 square kilometers of northern territory. Most of the other great falls owe their existence to the prodigious rains of the monsoon. A few actually dry up when the rains cease. In contrast, Niagara has the better part of the Great Lakes to draw from, a stupendous reservoir that contains more than 14,000 cubic kilometers of water.

Canadians are fond of reminding their Americans neighbors that Horseshoe Falls is bigger than the American Falls — a little too fond, perhaps; we can be braggarts at times. In return, Americans boast that their falls is higher — a little more than six feet higher. Ironically, that's the very reason Horseshoe Falls is so much bigger. Water flows downhill (as if you needed to be told), and nine times more of it goes over the lower, Canadian falls than the higher, American falls.

In the time it takes you to read this sentence, another million cubic feet of water will have gone over the brink of the three waterfalls we call Niagara. That's if you're reading it during daylight hours sometime between the beginning of April and the end of October; otherwise it's only half a million cubic feet. In the summer months the power companies in the two countries are allowed to divert half the regular flow of water after dark. In the winter months they can divert that amount 24 hours a day.

The pool at the bottom of Horseshoe Falls — to geologists it's a plunge pool, to the people of Niagara it's the Maid of the Mist Pool — is actually deeper than the Falls is high. The unceasing pounding of millions of tons of water has hollowed it out into a hideous place where few humans beings have ever gone and lived to tell about it.

You can appreciate how Niagara Falls came to exist if you know that the Escarpment is made up of layers, or strata, of rock that vary in their ability to resist erosion. We have this variance to thank for all the other waterfalls of the Escarpment.

The top layer, known as the caprock, is Lockport dolostone, a hard stone that has become infused at some point with magnesium. It is a beautiful building stone. It's also found in garden nurseries all over Southern Ontario, where it's sold to make elegant rock gardens.

Dolostone isn't easily eroded but Rochester shale is. That's the layer of stone immediately below the caprock. Water flowing over the edge of the Escarpment wears away this lower, softer stone and undermines the hard upper layer. The caprock is left suspended, with nothing but its own inherent strength to help it withstand the forces of gravity. Sooner or later it falls into the gorge below and

Niagara Falls moves a little further upstream. You can see great heaps of this "talus," as it is called, at the base of the American Falls. In 12,000 years, Niagara has "traveled" approximately 11 kilometers (about 7 miles) from where it began at Queenston.

So what appears to be unchanging isn't unchanging at all. The Falls is forever on the move, and not so slowly that its progress can't be observed and measured within a single lifetime. In the latter half of the 19th century, for example, Horseshoe Falls receded 104 feet in just 48 years.

In the middle of that century there were two spectacular vantage points from which to view the Falls — Prospect Point on the American side and Table Rock on the Canadian. Both have since disappeared. Table Rock was a formidable slab of caprock, more than an acre in size, which had hung suspended over the falling waters for centuries. Then one day in 1850, without warning, it cracked and collapsed into the gorge. In 1954, after some warning, most of Prospect Point split away and tumbled to the base of the American Falls.

The first European to set eyes on Niagara Falls, or at least the first to let the world know he had been there, was a Recollet priest, Louis Hennepin. Being in the right place at the right time earned him a footnote in history. Father Hennepin would never have described the largest of the waterfalls as horseshoe shaped, because in 1678 it wasn't. The crestline of what would later be called Horseshoe Falls was almost straight.

Three hundred years further back, about the time Good King Wenceslas ruled in Bohemia and Dante was busy writing *The Divine Comedy*, there was just one wide, enormous waterfall stretching across the gorge, at about the point where Bridal Veil Falls now is. At the time of Christ that single waterfall was a good way downstream, close to where the Rainbow Bridge now crosses the gorge.

In the ten millennia before that, the Falls must have taken on many different configurations. Dr. Walter Tovell is a much-honored Canadian geologist who has written about both the Escarpment and Niagara and is a kind of paterfamilias to all who cherish them. He has calculated that in the area we now call the Niagara Glen there very likely were three waterfalls, two upper falls separated by an island and a lower, larger falls. That was 8,000 to 9,000 years ago, at a time when the humans who were around may still have dined occasionally on mammoth or mastodon. We know just enough about that era to conjure up all kinds of fantasies.

And the Niagara Glen is a bewitching place to indulge those fantasies. It's on the gorge just north of the Whirlpool, not far from the botanical gardens and the floral clock. You have to climb down several flights of metal stairs to get to it, but once you're there, the going is relatively easy. It's a wonderland of trees and rock, rocks as big as houses and bigger. It's intersected by a maze of trails, none them especially long but several kilometers in aggregate. A number of these paths lead to the water's edge where you can find, among other fascinating things, White Medina sandstone, which comes from a desert that existed on this spot some 430 million years ago.

The American Falls up close and powerful.

The glen is unusual in that it's a kind of shelf halfway down the gorge. It was created when the waterfall nearest the American shore became low enough to draw water away from the one on the Canadian side and dry it up. The usual process of erosion, which cut out the gorge to its present depth, went uncompleted here.

The Niagara Glen is one of the most singularly fascinating places on the Escarpment, and yet most visitors to Niagara pass it by. It's the local people, from both sides of the border, who know it and frequent it.

Over the course of its long existence, Niagara Falls has slowly worked its way south toward Lake Erie at an average rate of one meter per year. Now humans have intervened to alter that. With diversions for power generation and alterations to the water flow, the rate of erosion may be down to one foot — every 10 years!

We were determined to find a fresh way of looking at Niagara Falls. The words "It's such a cliché" were still ringing in our ears, and we felt challenged. It took a while but we finally decided we would do as we had done with most of the other waterfalls and walk around it, observing and experiencing it from every reachable angle. That meant we were in for quite a walk, through parts of two countries.

Viewed from the Canadian side, the Falls present a sweeping panorama of splendor that never fails to leave visitors groping for adjectives. Viewing it from the American side, you find yourself caught up not in their grandeur but in their power.

(It's sometimes easier, incidentally, to enter the United States on foot than it is to get through the security screen in many office buildings and factories. We did fumble for change to feed the turnstiles on the Canadian side of the Rainbow Bridge and managed to come up with the necessary 50 cents each, without a penny to spare. There was no one around to make change.)

Our perspective began to change as we neared the center of the Rainbow Bridge. There, the river came into play and actually dominated the scene. What we could see from this new vantage point was a great river with three waterfalls in its midst.

The November sun was thin and intermittent. Every few minutes it would slip through the heavy overcast and its reflection would slide swiftly along the surface of the water from waterfall to waterfall. We were delighted. Niagara is so used to posing for the camera, so used to showing the world her best side. We felt we had somehow caught her unawares and in a sullen mood.

The customs officer on the American side saw the camera, asked what we were up to and then immediately lost interest in us. We pushed through the door next to him and to our surprise discovered we were not on a street in the city of Niagara Falls, New York, but in the tranquil setting of Niagara Falls State Park, the oldest (1885) and most-visited state park in the country. The American Falls was just a minute or two away. Over the next couple of hours we found that by crossing the bridges and islands that stretch the length of the park we were able to experience all three waterfalls in ways that are impossible on the distant Canadian shore.

When you stand at the crest of the American Falls, you can appreciate, as you can't from any other perspective, that it is really the explosive climax of a torturous journey that begins several hundred meters upstream. With water flow reduced to half during the winter months, the long stretch of rapids leading to the falls is much more exposed. The water appears to race past you that much faster. At the brink it almost seems to rise up and throw itself into the gorge.

We found ourselves staring right into the low, wintry sun as it cast its light across the surface of the churning water. (For the photographer who likes the difficult but often rewarding challenge of back lighting, this is as good as it gets.)

We crossed to Goat Island and worked our way down to tiny Luna Island. There we could stand between the American Falls and Bridal Veil Falls and feel the full force of both.

Bridal Veil tends to get lost in the spectacle of its gargantuan neighbors. If it existed at any other spot on the Escarpment, it would come into its own as one of the largest and one of the loveliest. It has its own engaging history. The first stairs into the gorge, the Biddle Stairs, were built down the side of Bridal Veil in 1829. People clambered up and down them for almost 100 years before the elevator was installed in 1925. A full five years after the stairs made going down into the gorge a relatively easy task, Joseph Ingramham, a young boy who lived nearby and who was obviously a bit more adventurous than his parents would have liked, discovered a large cave behind Bridal Veil. Everybody else who climbed down there to poke around missed it. It was a major attraction until the 1930s when a rock fall closed it off.

Luna Island, we were surprised to learn, gets its name from the fact that in the early 19th century, before there was artificial light to illuminate the night, visitors to the falls claimed they could see lunar rainbows arching from the falling water when the moon was especially bright. We have to accept their word for it and not assume that they were, well, a little "loony." The presence of artificial light makes it unlikely we will ever again see lunar rainbows over Bridal Veil Falls. Bridal Veil Falls, incidentally, has been known variously in the past as Luna Falls and Iris Falls.

It only took us minutes to cross Goat Island to the crest of the Canadian Falls. We were struck by the way the winter light gave an eerie, otherworldly look to the broad watery wastes above the Falls. A large part of the Canadian shore was obscured by the plume of spray that hung in the air, but from where we stood we could see well into the middle of the horseshoe. The crest, remember, is a little better than two thirds of a kilometer in length. Put all three waterfalls together and you have a crest width of more than a kilometer.

There's a more parklike atmosphere on this side of the Falls. A long grassy slope runs down to the water's edge and there's only a railing between you and the anxious waters at the brink. Viewed like this, without encumbrances, Niagara seems more powerful, more majestic than ever. You can actually sit on a park bench, just feet away, and let yourself be enthralled. And it being November, we weren't too shocked to find the bench unoccupied.

On the way back we had a closer look at some of the trees in the park. Thanks to several generations of stubborn visionaries, Goat Island has always been protected from the ravages of development. The trees are exceptional, including several large beech, a good number of mature tamarack, some enormous oak and maple and the largest gingko we had ever seen. We were especially taken with the old sycamores.

As we crossed back over the bridge we could see the new skyline of Niagara Falls growing up around the casino and the honky-tonk on Clifton Hill. As Canadians we found it quite a role change to return from the quiet, peacefulness of the United States to the garishness of home. It'll take some getting use to.

If you start at the crest of Horseshoe Falls on the Canadian side and walk all the way round to the crest on the American side and back again, you can count on a hike of about 8 kilometers. If you park your car near Rainbow Bridge, you can cut the round-trip distance to less than 6 kilometers.

For those whose hunger for information about Niagara is never satiated and who have access to the Internet, try Niagara Falls Thunder Alley (http://www.iaw.on.ca/~falls/). This is a beautifully designed website that's rich with data.

DeCew Falls

On Beaverdams Creek

UPPER FALLS
Height – 20 m (66 ft)　　　Crest Width – 14 m (45 ft)　　　N 43:06:82　W 79:15:91
LOWER FALLS
Height – 11 m (36 ft)　　　Crest Width – 5 m (16 ft)

Mountain Mills Museum

Best Time to View: All year round. Thanks to the little lakes that feed the nearby power plant and the adjacent waterworks, these are two waterfalls that never go dry. Both are curtain falls facing north and are relatively open to the sky.

Responsible Authority: St. Catharines Department of Recreation and Community Services, (905) 937-7210

How to Get There: Take the QEW to Exit 49 and travel south on Highway 406. This will take you through St. Catharines. Exit at St. David's Road and go right. In a short distance you'll come to the Merrittville Highway. Turn left. Another short drive will bring you to DeCew Road. Turn right. This lovely road will take you between Lakes Gibson and Moodie and past the ruins of the DeCew homestead. When you see the St. Catharines waterworks on your right get ready to turn in — the mill and the falls are just meters beyond that. There's parking for several cars.

It's appropriate that DeCew should be the first waterfall on the Escarpment west of Niagara Falls, because the contrast between the two couldn't be greater. While Niagara is awesome, colossal, overwhelming, DeCew is intimate, graceful and rustic.

This lovely waterfall and its homey surroundings look much as they must have 100 years ago — more so every day, in fact. The gristmill has been restored and is producing flour and cereals once again. The miller's house, which is just up the slope, has been renovated. They're going to rebuild the sawmill that once stood on the other side of the millpond, and they may reconstruct the blacksmith's forge that was at the head of the lane.

This is not some government scheme to create yet another pioneer village but a community project in which skilled volunteers have done most of the rebuilding and restored much of the equipment. They've found their inspiration in a simple love for this pretty waterfall and a romantic appreciation of the busy rural life that once surrounded it.

The little gristmill at DeCew was the second in Ontario to be driven by a turbine and may be the only one in the province that has never been powered by a waterwheel. There is a waterwheel on the other side of the falls, but that was built

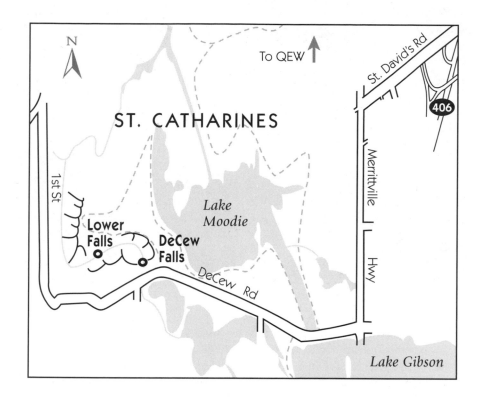

by the Friends of the Morningstar Mill in 1995 in anticipation of the rebuilding of the sawmill.

The original turbine is still functioning, still turning all the mill's shafts and gears and belts. You can find it down in the shed at the north end of the mill, at the crest of the falls, in a 40-foot pit chiseled out of solid rock. It's been churning there faithfully for over 125 years. Near it is an enormous wood lathe, big enough to turn the ends of a fence post. It, too, is run by waterpower.

The water to drive the turbine is drawn from the millpond, which was created when they quarried the stone to build the mill.

The mill gets its name from Wilson Morningstar, a Port Colborne farmer, who bought it from the city of St. Catharines in 1883. His family had been in Canada since 1792 and could trace its roots back through the Pennsylvania Dutch to Germany where their name was Morgenstern.

In an era that was rich with people who were good with their hands and capable of all kinds of innovations, Wilson Morningstar appears to have been cleverer than most. He incorporated many of his own inventions into the millworks and used unique systems for sifting whole wheat, buckwheat, flour and animal feed. Most of these devices are still part of the mill's operating equipment. When hydro-electric power came along and they were building the DeCew generating plant downstream from the falls, Morningstar was quick to grasp the concept and rig up

The lower falls at DeCew.

a generator to the mill's turbine so that he could produce power of his own. His was one of the first farmhouses in the Niagara Peninsula lit by electricity. (The people who have restored the mill estimate they could now generate power worth up to $500,000 a year, but to do so they would have to upgrade their operations to Ontario Hydro specifications and that would ruin the mill as a historic site.)

Morningstar wasn't without troubles and challenges. Fire, the scourge of all millers because grain and flour are so combustible, gutted the building soon after he bought it. Water, or the lack of it, was just as discouraging. Beaver Dams Creek wasn't a very sizable stream, and the St. Catharines waterworks had dammed it up and controlled the flow. His fortunes were reversed in the most dramatic manner with the rebuilding of the Welland Canal in 1887 and the construction of the hydro generating plant in 1898. These brought water all the way from Lake Erie, all the water he could ever want or use.

For 50 years, Wilson Morningstar operated what was, in retrospect, a 19th-century industrial complex, the kind of complex that existed at many of the waterfalls of the Escarpment. He had the gristmill and a sawmill that was powered by a shaft extended across the stream from the turbine. There were two blacksmiths and a carpentry shop, and a cider press that could turn out 1,800 gallons a day — at a penny a gallon! Not a lot of cash changed hands. Virtually all of the work he did was on a share basis. He kept 1/12 of everything he milled.

In his final years Morningstar no longer produced flour, only animal feed. Modern times caught up with him and millers everywhere. Bakeries began to sell freshly baked bread along with cakes and pies, delivered daily to one's door. Women no longer had to bake their own every day or two. And they no longer came to the mill to buy flour.

When Morningstar died in 1933, the mill ceased to operate. Ontario Hydro bought it and used it for storage. In 1962 the city of St. Catharines took it over and turned it into the Mountain Mills Museum. For years the miller's grandchildren, Don and Lorna Robson, looked after the place and acted as tour guides. In 1991, Don fell into the gorge one night and was killed. That tragic mishap brought to an end the saga of the Morningstar family's 108 years at DeCew Falls.

The St. Catharines Department of Recreation and Community Services had long wanted to restore the little mill, but the cost was always beyond its means. Finally, in 1992, a group of volunteers came forward to do the job — the Friends of the Morningstar Mill. Right behind them came the John Howard Society, to renovate Wilson Morningstar's classic five-bedroom Ontario farmhouse.

Even before we set eyes on it we found ourselves expecting DeCew Falls to be something different, something special. It had a lot to do with the land we passed through on the way to the falls, the passive little lakes and the quiet countryside surrounding them. To our eyes, at least, it looked more like a landscape you might find in the Southern United States than in Canada. However true that might seem to others, we decided the people of St. Catharines had themselves a treasure in a place so benign.

It was a perfect spring day and there wasn't a soul in sight. The door to the mill was open. Just inside, on an old chair, stood a big pickle jar. A slot had been punched in its metal top and a handwritten sign fixed to the back of the chair invited us to make a contribution to the restoration of the mill and the surrounding buildings. There were several loonies at the bottom of the jar…and, like I said, there was nobody around. What could be more welcoming than to be greeted with unquestioning trust.

We poked around on our own for some time before we found Gary Konkle, one of the Friends of the Morningstar Mill, in the blacksmith's shop. We spent a happy 20 minutes with him, talking about the work that had been done and the work still to be done. He impressed us most when he told us that they had saved a lot of money on new beams for the turbine shed by getting the Bell Telephone to drop off a load of used telephone poles, from which the Friends then cut the needed beams on a portable sawmill.

We made our second journey to DeCew in midwinter. This time there really was nobody around. There was a padlock on the door. That was okay — it gave us a chance to have a closer look at the falls and its surroundings. There was a bit of a thaw in the air and Mikal captured the feel of it perfectly with a picture he took after we gingerly crawled out onto the snowy edge of the gorge.

The third time back it was high summer again and we were in the mill with Greg Miller, the president of the Friends of the Morningstar Mill. The ever-present sound of the falls filled the air as we plied him with questions, which he answered in his unhurried manner. Then he stopped us with a question of his own.

"Have you seen the other falls?"

St. Catharine's historic DeCew Falls in late winter.

Other falls? What other falls? In all we had been told and all we had read, there had never been a hint about another waterfall at DeCew.

"It's just a short ways downstream from here," he said. "But you'll have to get down into the gorge if you want to see it."

We should have been thinking about lunch at that hour but the promise of finding a waterfall we hadn't even known existed was too much to put off. Following Greg's directions, we picked up the Bruce Trail where it passes behind the miller's house and walked along the ridge of the gorge away from the upper falls. It wasn't long before we could hear the lower falls, but we couldn't find a way to get down to it. (We were told later that there is no direct way down, though we saw evidence indicating that some people, probably the local teenagers, knew otherwise.)

We stayed on the trail, even as the sound of the elusive waterfall faded. We soon found ourselves descending but still heading away from our destination. About halfway down we decided to turn back toward the falls and work our way down to the level of the creek. From that point on the going was a bit rough. The sides of the gorge were steep and unstable. We weren't especially afraid of taking a tumble and falling downhill but we were concerned about setting off a landslide in the loose shale. We could hear the falls again as we got closer. That's the thrill of it — the sound of it, the anticipation you feel as you approach a waterfall you've never seen before.

And this one was worth the effort — a thousand times over! What a beauty! We stood there looking up at it, marveling at the prodigious volume of water coming at us. We had expected something meek and diminutive.

We climbed back up the slope to the brink where we found we could get safely and comfortably quite close to it. We watched the water flow darkly over the rocks just inches from our feet and then explode in liquid sunshine as it cleared the crest. The water in this waterfall didn't fall — it flew through the air. The space all around us sparkled in a crystalline radiance.

We were standing at the center of one of the most heavily populated areas in North America. Between seven and eight million people live within 100 kilometers of the Escarpment. Our car wasn't more than five minutes away as the crow flies. In ten minutes we could be sitting down ordering a beer and a pizza at the big roadhouse on the Merrittville Highway. And yet we couldn't have felt more remote from the clamorous world around us if we'd been in Algonquin Park. The sound of the falls eliminated the sound of everything else. Its beauty was so assertive, so mesmerizing, it was impossible to think of anything else.

When we finally stood up to leave, it was to walk further upstream to get a look at the upper falls from down below. The path was well trodden. Somebody, probably the teens we'd speculated about, definitely did have their own shortcut way of getting down here. Still, I could see the distinctive leaves of hepatica, the shyest of all spring flowers, peeking out unharmed from under the ferns at our feet.

We had read that at one time people used to come over from Toronto by steamer and then by radial car to spend the day at DeCew Falls. Some were said to have preferred it to Niagara. Now, looking at the upper falls, with the little mill hanging precariously on the crest of it and the midafternoon sun smiling down through the trees, we could finally appreciate why. If there was anything to match the exultant pleasure of discovering the lower falls, it was the sight of the upper falls, at this time of day, from this point of view. Mikal had the advantage over me, he was able to capture with his camera what I could never hope to express with words.

In the old days, Wilson Morningstar built a spiral stairway down into the gorge, for the convenience of the daytrippers from Toronto as much as for himself. It rotted away long ago but is finally going to be replaced by a steel stairway that will descend from the Bruce Trail at a point facing the falls. That will give people easier access to both waterfalls and save the sides of the gorge from the kind of damage that brings on erosion.

There's actually a third waterfall at DeCew. It's 50 meters or so to the east of the upper falls, a pretty little cascade that splashes effortlessly down the stony steps of the Escarpment. It's only when you climb to the brink that you discover its source is not some tiny tributary of Beaverdams Creek but concrete pipes set in the rocky wall. The Friends of the Morningstar Mill had prepared us for this. They laughingly call it Faucet Falls because it flows solely at the whim of the people in the waterworks next door. When we started out on this venture we decided to exclude dams and manmade waterfalls. We've stuck to that rule and not included Faucet Falls on our list, though if we were going to make an exception this would be it. It's a lovely addition to one of the Escarpment's most enchanting places.

DeCew Falls had a history long before the arrival of Wilson Morningstar. Almost a hundred years before him, John DeCew was milling flour here, largely to feed the British troops stationed at Niagara. His mill was not at the falls but at some long-lost spot to the east that has since been flooded over by Lakes Moodie and Gibson.

DeCew was descended from French Huguenots who fled to England in the 1600s. The name was sometimes spelled DeCou, even DeCow. Most sources say he was a United Empire Loyalist but one more intriguing story tells that he came from New Jersey in 1787 to work as a surveyor and found the wilderness of the Niagara Peninsula so compelling he decided to stay. He was especially taken with the waterfall on Beaver Dams Creek and bought the surrounding 100 acres from the Mississauga natives, so the story goes, for an axe and a blanket. He soon bought a second 100 acres from them for a gold doubloon.

DeCew prospered, married Katherine Docksettler, daughter of a Loyalist who had been a member of Butler's Rangers during the American Revolution, and fathered 11 children. He was soon known far and wide for his innovative skills as a farmer, fruit grower and industrialist as well as a miller. DeCew Town grew up around his gristmill and sawmill.

Most of all, DeCew was known for the superb stone house he built for his growing family in 1812. It was to this house that the stolid but intrepid Laura Secord made her overnight trek from Queenston in 1813 to warn the British that the

Americans were coming. DeCew was not in the house at the time. He was a militia captain and had been taken prisoner early in the war.

Today only the foundation of the house remains, destroyed not in the War of 1812 but 138 years later when it burned down after being expropriated by Ontario Hydro. What's left is the historic site on DeCew Road, just to the east of the falls.

When the war was over, DeCew joined friends and fellow millers George Keefer and the inestimable William Hamilton Merritt in conceiving plans to build the Welland Canal. The dream died for DeCew when the route of the canal was changed and threatened to dry up the water sources for his mills. He sold out and left town, no doubt with some bitterness, to resettle in Haldimand County. There he founded a new little community, DeCewsville, where he died in 1855.

Another captivating bit of history concerns the construction of the power plant, DeCew Falls No.1, as Ontario Hydro now calls it. The first plan was to build it right at the falls. Luckily for us and for the company's shareholders, they found a better spot further east where they could drop the water an extra 75 feet and produce additional kilowatts. Otherwise, there'd be no DeCew Falls to photograph or write about.

It was here at DeCew, not at Niagara, that they built Canada's first major hydroelectric power station. It was one of the first high-head hydraulic developments in the country, indeed, in the world.

And it was from here, not Niagara, that power was first transmitted over long-distance lines in Canada. For some reason a lot of people initially believed that electricity died on the line after 12 miles. And some of the most respected scientists of the age, including Thomas Edison and Lord Kelvin, believed it could only be transmitted by direct current. However, a young genius from Croatia, Nikola Tesla, believed otherwise and he convinced the Westinghouse Company to go with alternating current. In 1896 they successfully transmitted power from Niagara to Buffalo.

Edison still had a lot of people convinced that he was right when a year later, in 1897, a group of men from Hamilton formed the Cataract Power Company and put their money on Tesla. They were known amusingly as the "Five Johns" because they all had the same first name. In a little over 10 months they constructed a canal to bring Lake Erie water all the way from Allanburg, strung power lines from DeCew to Hamilton along the Grand Trunk right of way, and built and equipped a first-class power plant that is still in operation today. The original generators and turbines functioned for decades and the water intake system wasn't replaced until 1985.

On the afternoon of August 28, 1898, the flip of a switch instantly lit the lights and sent machines whirling 56 kilometers away in Hamilton. Soon power from DeCew was lighting streets and homes from St. Catharines to Brantford to Oakville. It's an astonishing, seldom-told story of business foresight and courage, a story of men who dared to risk all by riding the leading edge of new technology. None of the current tales about the pioneers of cyberspace is any more exciting than this one.

Swayze Falls

Tributary of Twelve Mile Creek

Height – 14 m (45 ft)   Crest Width – 6 m (20 ft)   N 43:07:86 W 79:17:12

Short Hills Provincial Park

Best Time to View: Fall through spring, especially during spring runoff or after a heavy snow melt. It's in moderately heavy woods and partially shaded. It's a steep, almost vertical cascade facing south.

Responsible Authority:

Ministry of Natural Resources, Ontario Parks, 1-800-667-1940

How to Get There: Take the QEW to Exit 49 and go south on Highway 406. This will take you through St. Catharines. Exit at St. David's Road and go right. In a short distance you'll come to the Merrittville Highway. Turn left. Another short drive will bring you to DeCew Road. Turn right. Follow this road past the St. Catharines waterworks, past DeCew Falls. Soon it will take a turn to the

At the crest of Swayze Falls.

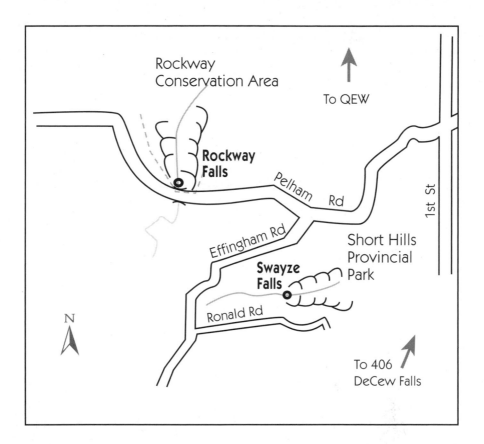

north and become 1st Street. Don't let that throw you! Keep going! In about a kilometer you'll come to Pelham Road. Turn left. Go a short distance to Effingham Road. Turn left again. Go south approximately 3 kilometers to Ronald Road. Make one last turn to the left. This will take you to the south parking lot of Short Hills Provincial Park, which is on your left. It's about a five-minute walk to the falls. As you enter the park, be sure to take the path to the right. It's wheelchair accessible, though just barely. Wheelchair accessible means it's also stroller accessible.

We were standing on a viewing platform, suspended over the gorge, admiring the pristine beauty of a waterfall we hadn't known existed until we saw a passing reference to it in a tourist brochure.

Soft yellow rays of the autumn sun were streaming through the trees, catching the long silky threads of water as they fell and reaching deep into the shadows at the bottom of the narrow, crevice-like gorge. The quality of light was exquisite.

Our only companion on the platform was an interesting-looking man who wore a cloth cap and a close-cut, neatly trimmed beard. He was somehow managing to keep one eye on the waterfall and the other on his two children, a toddler who clung precariously to a stroller and a little girl who was trying her best to slip away and explore this bright, dangerous place. We admired the way he coolly kept control, without spoiling the experience for the children or himself.

Swayze Falls, we learned, was one of his favorite spots; he came by at least once a week. It didn't bother him that there weren't tons of water thundering over its brink. It didn't bother us either. The falls has a kind of cool, spring-like purity to it that's just right for the setting, though our companion did say it had been spectacular the previous January when a 40-centimeter snowfall melted away almost as fast as it had fallen.

He introduced himself as a retired chef and restaurant owner from St. Catharines. He looked too young to be retired. He told us he had sacrificed every waking hour to his business for 20 years. Now he stayed home and kept house and looked after the kids while his wife went out to work. I asked him how he liked being a househusband. He answered with a quick, inscrutable smile.

He knew the Niagara part of the Escarpment well and was familiar with some of the waterfalls around Hamilton. He urged us to visit the spruce forest at St. John's, which is just south of Short Hills. He went there often, he told us, to observe the wild turkeys, and had once come upon nearly 20 of them roosting in the lower branches of the trees.

We envied his closeness to all this. He envied the family that had once lived next to this lovely waterfall. He pointed to a place in the clearing, just beyond the trees, where the house had stood.

As we were leaving we stopped to look south over the open, rolling meadowland. The woods on either side were aflame with fall color and there was a hint of coolness in the air. How perfect, I thought, to have all this at your doorstep, to go with your very own waterfall.

Rockway Falls

On Fifteen Mile Creek

Height – 19.5 m (63 ft)   Crest Width – 4.5 m (15 ft)   N 43:07:78   W 79:17:16

Rockway Falls Conservation Area

Best Time to View: Fall through spring. There are series of rapids and smaller falls above and below the main falls. All show best when there's lots of water. It's spectacular in winter. Rockway faces north but it's in the sun through the middle of day. This is a cascade.

Responsible Authority:

Niagara Peninsula Conservation Authority, (905) 788-3135

How to Get There: Take the QEW to Exit 49 and go south on Highway 406. This will take you through St. Catharines. Exit at St. David's Road and go right. In a short distance you'll come to the Merrittville Highway. Turn left. Another short drive will bring you to DeCew Road. Turn right. Follow this road past the St. Catharines waterworks, past DeCew Falls. Soon it will take a turn to the north and become 1st Street. Don't let that confuse you! Keep going! In about a kilometer you'll come to Pelham Road. Turn left. Rockway Falls is on this road, approximately 4 kilometers from this intersection. Don't look for a sign to tell you that you're there. There isn't one. Look instead for a small community center on your right and pull into the parking lot. The falls is in the gorge behind the center.

You could drive over the bridge on Pelham Road every day of your life and not know there's a magnificent waterfall beneath you. It's not because it's small. If you take the main falls together with several smaller companion waterfalls, you've got one of the best water shows on the Escarpment. It has character! If you've been to Rome, then try to imagine Fifteen Mile Creek pouring down the Spanish Steps.

It's the gorge, not the falls, that's deceiving. It's cut so deeply and abruptly into the face of the Escarpment that it looks like just another bit of woods to someone passing by in a car.

The west side of the gorge is one long, straight drop to the water. In fact, if you venture to the edge of some of the overhangs, you'll find yourself peering directly into the rapids below. It's not a place for those who have a fear of heights.

On the east side, near the falls, the gorge is equally precipitous, but downstream it gives way to a sloping bank of shale that goes down to the water's edge. That's the shortest way to the bottom. You get to it by taking a path that begins behind the community center and following it until you come to a spot where you can conveniently get down to a second path that runs along the face of the gorge

A swift descent at Rockway Falls.

and takes you back to the falls. The journey is safe enough if you take reasonable care, but again, it's not a place to be if you are afraid of heights.

Down below, at the base of the falls, we found proof that the dolostone overhangs bordering the gorge do come tumbling down from time to time. The stream was littered with freshly broken blocks of caprock, tons of it. We could tell they had fallen recently because their newly opened surfaces were lovely soft shades of cream and beige. Moss and lichens and the weather hadn't had a chance to alter them yet. It was intriguing to realize that the interior of the stone had just been exposed to air and wind and sun for the first time in more than 400 million years.

As you climb back up the gorge and work your way along the ledge of rock at the top, you can see to the north where Rockway Glen widens and then gives way to the vineyards of the Niagara Peninsula. If it's a clear day, you'll be able to see much beyond that, across the waters of Lake Ontario to the CN Tower and Sky-Dome and the buildings of Bay Street.

Louth Falls

On Sixteen Mile Creek

Height – 9 m (30 ft)   Crest Width – 6.5 m (21 ft)   N 43:07:23 W 79:21:26

Louth Conservation Area

Best Time to View: In early spring or after a winter thaw or a period of heavy rain. This is a series of small waterfalls and rapids that tend to dry up completely in summer. They face north and are mostly under forest cover.

Responsible Authority:

Niagara Peninsula Conservation Authority, (905) 788-3135

How to Get There: Take the QEW to Exit 57 (Vineland). Turn right onto Victoria Avenue (Niagara Road 24). It will take you up the Escarpment. Keep on this road till you come to 7th Avenue. Turn left. Travel about 3 kilometers to 17th Street. (Sounds as if you're in Lower Manhattan, doesn't it?) Turn right. Almost immediately you'll see a little road bearing off to the left. Follow it. Just ahead, on your left, is Louth Conservation Area. There's parking for four or five cars. You can access the Bruce Trail from the parking lot. It will take you along Sixteen Mile Creek and past the waterfall.

It was the third year of the worst drought since the 1930s and we were in the midst of a long dry spell. We weren't expecting much as we pulled up under the dusty trees on the edge of Louth Conservation Area. We could see Sixteen Mile Creek where it crossed the cow pasture on the other side of the road. It was dry. The big gray rocks in the stream bed looked like a family of slumbering elephants baking in the sun.

With the little stream having vanished, we knew the falls would be gone too. We followed the creek into the woods and, to our surprise, found a small waterfall just steps from the road. There was a brackish-looking pool of brown water at its base and nothing more. Not one drop of falling water!

Nothing, we decided, is more difficult to appreciate than a waterfall that has no water in it. Even the rocks over which the water would normally flow are uninteresting. They lack the natural look of the stone on the surrounding walls of the gorge, cloaked as it is in moss and lichens. If there's any green to be found on the rocks of a waterfall gone dry, it's usually the ugly verdure of algae, not the earthy verdancy of moss. Still, we did what any two optimists would do and tried to imagine what the little falls would look like when once again it had water rushing at its brink. Small as it is — it's only 8 to 10 feet high — we imagined it would be quite charming.

The fence that surrounded the property at one time was no longer evident. An old metal farm gate stood there alone. It was open. Obviously farm wagons used

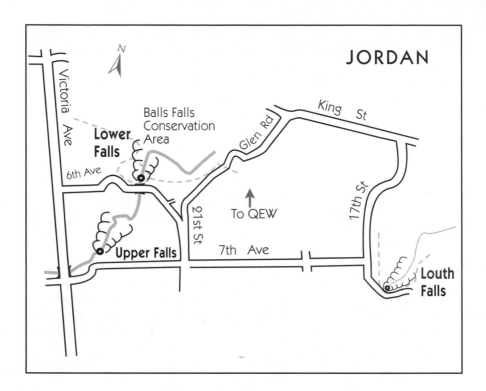

to come and go here. Judging by the size of the trees that now impeded the forlorn-looking gate, whoever walked away from the place for the last time did so a long time ago, feeling it was no longer important to pull the gate shut behind him.

We discovered another branch of the little creek a short distance to the east. It flowed through a series of rapids after entering the woods. We ventured onto a large, smooth slab of dolostone. There had been a bit of a waterfall here once, but the stream had undermined the caprock and it now flowed under rather than over it. Or so we guessed. The creek was as dry here as elsewhere. As we stood there, trying to imagine what the place would look like with water flowing through it, we spied what appeared to be the footprint of a large bird in the surface of the big block of stone lying just down stream of us. We made a rush for it, though we realized almost before we got to it that it couldn't be. The sedimentary rock that is the topmost strata of the Escarpment was formed from the soft bottom of a shallow sea that existed on this spot more than 400 million years ago. There were no birds then. There were no land creatures.

The "footprint" certainly looked real enough but we guessed it to be a coincidental scarring left behind after the Wisconsin Glacier scraped across the surface of this rock 15 or 20 thousand years ago. That, we knew was plausible. At times that colossal sheet of ice grew to be 2 or 3 kilometers thick. It was certainly capable of leaving its mark on the hardest rock surface.

I ran my hand over the smooth surface of the stone, enjoying its coolness. What an exciting place to bring young children, I thought. Here's a part of the Escarpment that's on a very human scale. Even with water in the stream, it would still be accessible and they could climb about on the rocks in relative safety. And if a parent came prepared with a little knowledge, enough at least to answer questions in an elementary way, he or she or they could make it a more edifying experience than any book, film, classroom lesson or television program.

As I was thinking this, I was suddenly struck by the irony that here I was with my own son, who long ago reached manhood, and I was the one who usually begged for answers.

Mine is an ordinary curiosity when it comes to nature. Mikal appreciates it on a more knowledgeable, more imaginative level. He can visualize the ancient sea that existed here and appreciate what a rich Silurian soup it must have been, with uncountable numbers of tiny shell creatures and great coral reefs. He can appreciate that those little beings still have a physical presence on Earth, for their fossilized remains form an integral and not inconsiderable part of the rock itself.

Seeing the dried-up rapids and that little waterfall without water was like entering an empty theater and seeing a stage setting with only the house lights to illuminate it. There was no magic. And there really is something magical about a waterfall. We made a promise to watch the calendar and come back when the rains returned. We were anxious to explore further downstream but not until Sixteen Mile Creek was back to its old self.

Balls Falls

On Twenty Mile Creek

LOWER FALLS
Height – 27 m (88 ft)   Crest Width – 38.5 m (125 ft)   N 43:07:94 W 79:23:03
UPPER FALLS
Height – 11 m (36 ft)   Crest Width – 20 m (65 ft)   N 43:07:77 W 79:22:72

Balls Falls Conservation Area

Best Time to View: Fall through early summer. Midseason drought will diminish these waterfalls considerably. Both face north but are open to the sky. The lower falls is a curtain falls; the upper is a near vertical cascade.

Responsible Authority:
Niagara Peninsula Conservation Authority, (905) 788-3135

How to Get There: Take the QEW to Exit 57 (Vineland). Turn right onto Victoria Avenue (Niagara Road 24). It will take you south to the Escarpment. Keep on this road till you reach 6th Avenue. There you'll see the sign for Balls Falls Conservation Area and Historical Park. Turn left. A brief drive will take you right into the conservation area grounds. There's plenty of parking. Expect to pay an entry fee in season.

If you've never experienced the Niagara Escarpment, never walked its long, lovely trails or stopped to admire the splendid trees and soaring rock walls, or stood in awe of its graceful waterfalls, this is a beguiling place to begin the acquaintance. All the better if you choose one of those exquisite days in late fall, perhaps a little after Thanksgiving, when there are fewer people around and the trees are still wearing their reddest reds and sunniest yellows and fresh rains have brought the waterfalls back to sparkling perfection.

Visit the upper falls first, and do it by crossing the bridge to the trail on the west bank of Twenty Mile Creek. You'll soon find yourself in the woods on an old cart track, heading south up a long, gentle slope. In a minute or two you'll come to a substantial outcropping of mossy stone, the ever-present distinguishing mark of the Escarpment. From this point on, all the way to the falls, the creek bed is littered with pieces of caprock, some of them huge. One especially large piece rests on it side, at a defiant angle, daring gravity to pull it down. It's a fair guess that it has been there for centuries.

If there's a lot of water in the creek, Upper Ball's Falls will take you by surprise. It's exceptionally beautiful. Because of its size and proximity to the historical buildings and the picnic grounds, the lower falls gets most of the attention but the upper falls is far from small and it has much more character.

Upper Balls in fall.

It's unusual, too. Somehow a considerable volume of water has found its way around the falls and worked in under the caprock on the far edge of the gorge, creating what is almost a separate waterfall. There's nothing on the Escarpment quite like it. The caprock itself, which is crowned by a number of mature trees, looks treacherously unstable. A well-placed chain-link fence prevents visitors from venturing too near the edge. There's no way someone standing on top of it would know how dangerous it is. When it does finally collapse into the gorge, the falls will likely take on a horseshoe shape, with a bit of an island in the middle of it.

Close to the near bank, a similar piece of caprock has already fallen into the gorge and taken a couple of big trees and a lilac bush with it. Surprisingly, all three are alive and in leaf.

It's not unusual to find lilacs at the bottom of this or any other gorge on the Escarpment. The crests of many waterfalls are crowded with them. They're there not because they have any special affinity for these locations but because people planted them there.

Lilacs are able to sucker and develop into clumps but they lack the ability to spread further on their own. For centuries they've depended on humans to take them to the four corners of the world. The Persians, who spread their love of gardens throughout the Mediterranean along with the word of Islam, were the ones who rescued the lilac from obscurity in the mountains of Southeast Asia. The perfume in the perfumed Persian garden came in large part from the flowers of the lilac.

The shrub had one other essential quality. The Persian garden was a spring garden. When the torrid summer set in, almost everything dried up and withered away except the lilacs. There wasn't a summer hot enough to kill them. Centuries later, Europeans found it to be just as hardy in the fiercest of winters.

When the early settlers crossed the Atlantic to North America they somehow found a place among their meager belongings for lilacs. When the United Empire Loyalists fled the terrors of the American Revolution, often with little more than the clothes on their backs, they nevertheless brought their lilacs with them. It is the Loyalists who planted the lilacs at the waterfalls in the lower parts of the Escarpment. And you won't find them growing any thicker than they do around Upper Ball's Falls.

Once you've found a path to take you through the lilacs you'll discover that you can walk out onto the crest of the falls and stand quite safely at the water's edge. Upstream, Twenty Mile Creek is the picture of serenity as it meanders through cow pastures and cornfields. It's only when it reaches the falls that the outcroppings of rock appear. The Escarpment is really the edge of a much larger, saucer-shaped geological formation. Standing there at the falls you are standing on its exposed rim.

When you make your way back downstream, stop at the ruins of the old woolen mill, which is less than 100 meters from the upper falls. It was built by George Ball in 1824 and used water diverted from the falls to power machinery that made tweeds and flannels and other fabrics. It ceased operation in 1882, surviving for almost 60 years, longer than all but the most venerable companies of our own time.

This is an enchanting spot with sizable trees having grown up since then, some of them inside the old mill walls. It gives every appearance of having been a pleasant little building to work in, tucked away in the quiet of the woods. How deceiving the passage of time can be. How deceiving a few mossy old stone walls can be. At the lower falls, in the big barn next to the gristmill, there's a photograph of the woolen mill on the wall and it's a shocker. The building was huge. Five stories high, with the biggest, ugliest chimney you ever saw. There isn't a tree to be seen. The whole side of the gorge is bare. They had cut down everything.

We forget how much the early settlers hated trees. They couldn't get rid of them fast enough. Have a look at some of the other photos in the barn. Glen Elgin, as the community clustered around the lower falls was called, was a barren-looking place. Not only was it treeless but the houses were unpainted, unkempt-looking structures. Some look as if they were ready to collapse. The old photos don't lie. Many of the early settlements were dreadful places. What you see at Ball's Falls today is an idealized community. It's a far more inviting place now than it ever was in the sentimentalized past.

In admiring the upper falls so unreservedly, we don't mean to disparage the lower one. It's big and quite magnificent when it has a full head of water at its crest. The adjacent mill, though it no longer operates, is an interesting building. It's one of the last of the old mills still standing, even more rare because it is constructed not of stone but of well-weathered clapboard.

The other buildings preserved in the village are equally interesting, especially the large, elegant brick home that belonged to M. A. Ball, who was a lawyer. It obviously was built sometime after the earlier hovels either burned or were torn down or fell down.

Most fascinating of all is the Fairchild cabin, which stands next to the Ball house. Peering through the doorway you can see that it consists of just one room, a room about the size of the living room in an average modern home. It contains a table and chairs, a double bed and a cradle, and not much more save for the enormous fireplace. In a space that small the settlers somehow were able to raise 10 or 12 children or more, all of them born in the bed in corner. Mealtimes must have been chaos with that many hungry children, each of them wielding a wooden spoon to dig food out of a communal bowl. All but the babies slept in the low, cramped space in the loft above. You can imagine them snuggling together like piglets for warmth in the cold of winter.

If that number of children in one family sounds like an exception rather than the rule, consider that Jacob Ball, the Loyalist who gave his name to the waterfalls, had 11 children. His eldest son also had 11. And the eldest sons in the next two generations had 9 each.

The original settlers were sometimes reluctant to leave their log cabins, even when they had the means to build a home as substantial as that occupied by the Balls. It was the second and third generations who built the sturdy farmhouses still seen on the country roads of Ontario. Some in the first generation actually preferred to go on living in their cabins.

You can appreciate why they might feel that way if you look again at the interior of the Fairchild cabin. It's really a very cozy place, especially for an old couple left alone at last, their children all grown up and gone,

One of Canada's early rustic poets, William Wye Smith (1827–1917), wrote a verse about such a couple, a couple who felt so out of place living in their big new brick home they decided to return to their pioneer beginnings. Here's a bit of "The Second Concession of Deer."

But John was hickory to the last,
On the second concession of Deer!
And out on the river end of his lot
He laid up the logs in a cozy spot,
And self and wife took up with a cot,
And the great brick house might swim or not
He was done with the pride of Deer!

Thirty Mile Creek Falls

On Thirty Mile Creek

Height – 15 m (49 ft)   Crest Width – 2.5 m (8 ft)   N 43:10:07 W 79:30:91

Best Time to View: Late fall or early spring or after a period of heavy rain. The falls face northeast and are shaded by moderately heavy woods. Don't be mis-led by the height of 15 meters; it's really a series of small ribbon falls separated by rapids.

Responsible Authority: The Bruce Trail Association, (905) 529-6821

How to Get There: Take the QEW to Exit 68 (Grimsby). You'll find yourself on Bartlett Avenue. Go south a short distance to King Street. Turn left. Go east a couple of kilometers to 30 Road (Niagara County Road 514). Turn right. This will take you up the Escarpment. As you near the top, you should see on your right the white sign marking the Bruce Trail. If you miss it, go to the top of the Escarpment where 30 Road meets Ridge Road and turn around and come back. The trail is about 100 meters down from that intersection. The falls are another 100 meters in from the road to the west. There's room to park just one car where the Bruce Trail crosses 30 Road.

"The trail crosses the road, goes down a track into a wooded area, turns right and crosses 30 Mile Creek at a small waterfall." That's all it said, just two lines in the *Bruce Trail Guide*, but it was enough to send us searching for a waterfall that appeared to have no name.

It was spring, about a week before the trees leafed out, and for once we didn't hear the roar of falling water until we were right on top of the falls. We felt some disappointment as we crossed the creek. From that angle it didn't look like much at all. But as we made our way along the path on the far side we realized we had discovered a little gem, or rather a series of little gems. It wasn't one waterfall but a string of them, tumbling primly, one into the other, all the way to the bottom of the deep V-shaped gorge.

We worked our way cautiously down the slope till we found a spot where Mikal could shoot between the trees and capture at least a part of this marvelous run of water. Alas, the camera chose that day to act up. No matter, we told our-selves, we'd get our pictures next time.

It was only a few weeks till next time, but what a metamorphosis. Our charm-ing little collection of waterfalls had dried up into a gully full of rocks.

We tried again in early fall. Once more the water was flowing but nothing like it had been in early spring. It was enough, however, to bring back some of the magic. We took time to have a good look around. It seemed the kind of place that

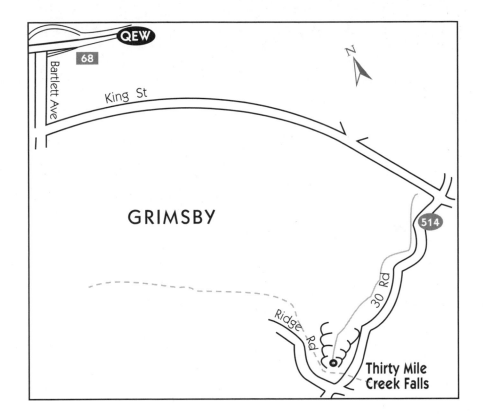

would meet the approval of young children. It has that intimate, secret-place-in-the-woods kind of feel to it.

There are several spots across the gorge where the caprock is suspended in midair, producing what any child with imagination will instantly recognize as caves, caves in which aboriginal people or trappers or explorers might had bedded down for the night two or three centuries ago. Who's to say that some of them didn't come this way that long ago and do precisely that.

One overhang extends out at least 10 or 12 feet into the middle of absolutely nothing. You could certainly spend the night under that one, though probably with some apprehension as you wondered if the rock would pick that moment of all the moments in eternity to give up the ghost and fall down and squash you — a wonderfully scary scenario.

There are several big trees on the other side that have so contorted their roots they've completely enclosed some of the larger rocks. They look like some species of woodland octopus.

There's nothing so wild on the near side of the gorge, though Mikal did discover what appeared to be a fox's den just below the path. There were neat entrances on both sides of a small outcropping of rock. And there was a fresh-looking tuft of fur just inside one of them, no doubt the remnants of dinner from the night before.

We returned to the car reluctantly. It would be a long wait till the spring runoff brought the little run of waterfalls back to perfection.

On the day we found the falls at Thirty Mile Creek dry we also found Beamer's dry. That was a bigger disappointment. Beamer's is no small waterfall. When there's lots of water it's a thundering cascade.

We had been there before, a number of times. In spring it put on a spectacular show, in winter it was magnificent, especially when the low February sun caught the edges of the ice floes at just the right angle and made them glisten in all the colors of the spectrum. All that greeted us now was an ugly green carpet of that most unwelcome of growing things, algae. The sight of it made us appreciate, as we never had before, just how much character and distinctiveness the waterfalls bring to the Escarpment. Without them it's a far lesser place. Susanna Moodie was right: "By night and day, in sunshine or in storm, water is always the most sublime feature in a landscape, and no view can be truly grand in which it is wanting."

It was still early in the year; it was only June. The birds were still mating. Down in the gorge a gang of blue jays was squabbling with more than the usual hysteria. A flicker was struggling mightily to raise his voice above the racket. Without the sound of the falls, Mikal observed, it was more like an Amazon forest than Carolinian forest.

Beamer's Falls

On Forty Mile Creek

Height – 12 m (39 ft)　　　　Crest Width – 8 m (26 ft)　　　　N 43:10:79　W 79:34:64

Beamer Memorial Conservation Area

Best Time to View: Fall through spring. Summer drought will dry up Beamer's. However, it can be an exceptional sight in winter thanks to the mix of ice and water. It faces northeast and is open to the sky. This is a long cascade.

Responsible Authority:

Niagara Peninsula Conservation Authority, (905) 788-3135

How to Get There: Take the QEW to Exit 71 (Grimsby). You'll find yourself on Christie Street. Go south. Along the way, Christie Street will become Mountain Street. Keep on going, nevertheless, till you reach the top of the Escarpment. Turn right onto Ridge Road. You'll find the falls on your right, less than a kilometer away. There's no guardrail and Beamer's is so close to the road that you could, if you wanted to, easily drive your car over the edge of the gorge and go for a tumble down the cascade. Don't! Park it instead. There's space for several cars.

The crest of Beamer's Falls in early spring.

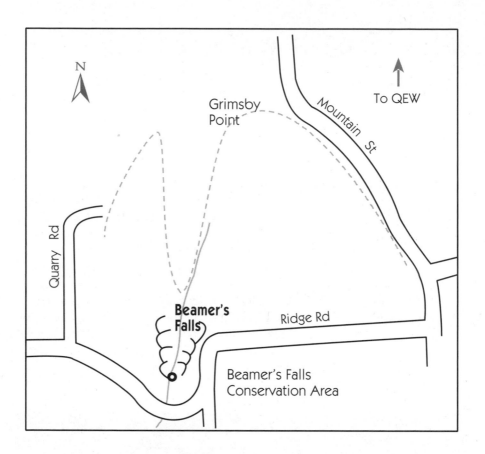

Quarry Road is just west of the falls, off Ridge Road. The Bruce Trail crosses it just a few meters north of Ridge Road. Look for the white sign and pick up the trail heading east. It will soon take you out to famous Grimsby Point and a spectacular view of Lake Ontario. Below you, on a narrow ledge, some of the finest vinifera grapes are grown. They thrive in a microclimate created by the Escarpment.

From Grimsby Point the trail loops back south, along the rim of the gorge, and then north again along the bank of Forty Mile Creek. Eventually you'll come to Mountain Street. That's a good turnaround point. You'll have gone a couple of kilometers by the time you retrace your steps. Allowing time to stop and have a look at things, the walk should take you about 45 minutes to an hour.

The Devil's Punch Bowl

On Stoney Creek

UPPER FALLS
Height – 34 m (110 ft)   Crest Width – 3 m (10 ft)   N 43:12:08 W 79:45:63

LOWER FALLS
Height – 5 m (16 ft)   Crest Width – 6 m (19.5 ft)

The Devil's Punch Bowl Conservation Area

Best Time to View: Prolonged rainy periods in fall and winter and spring thaw are the only times you're likely to see substantial water coming over this waterfall. The rocky strata of the Escarpment is the attraction here. The upper falls is open to the sky; the lower is shaded by woods. Both face north, and both are ribbon falls.

Responsible Authority:
Hamilton Region Conservation Authority, (905) 648-4427

How to Get There: Take the QEW to Exit 88 (Stoney Creek). You'll find yourself on Centennial Parkway (Hamilton-Wentworth Road 20). Go south through Stoney Creek and up the Escarpment. Just as you reach the top you'll come to Ridge Road. Turn left. It's easy to miss, so stay in the left lane and keep your eyes open. Ridge Road will take you to the upper falls in less than a minute. There's a parking lot on the east side.

This isn't a very impressive waterfall. Even in the spring, when water levels are high, it doesn't put on a very good show. Stoney Creek isn't much to get excited about either. In earlier times people would have called this little stream a rill or a run. At best you'll find barely enough water in it to float a canoe. But don't let any of that discourage you. This is a fascinating place. Don't miss it!

The gorge here is enormous, far too big to have been made by the little stream that currently flows over its edge. Sixteen thousand years ago, a powerful waterfall, fed by the prodigious meltwaters of the Wisconsin Glacier, scoured out this symmetrical rocky bowl with deft precision.

The use of the name "punch bowl" is far from whimsical. Punch bowl is a term occasionally used to describe what once was the plunge pool of an ancient waterfall. When you peer into the depths of this bowl you're looking back more than 400 million years, at history captured in stone and laid out layer on neat layer, like the pages in a book. Some of these layers were once the sediment at the bottom of a tropical sea. What we now see and recognize as dolostone and limestone are in large part the fossilized remains of the coral and shell creatures that died in that sea.

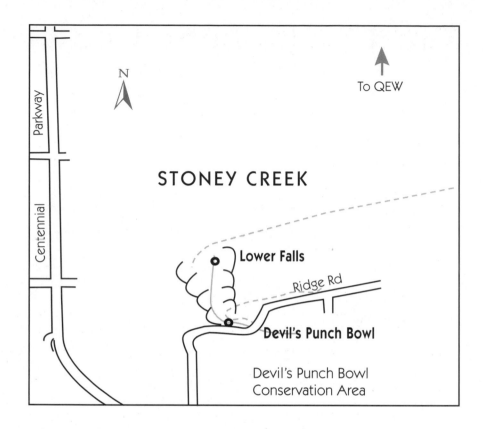

As you work your way along the rim of this great bowl and come to edge of the Escarpment, you'll find yourself at a lookout with a large illuminated steel cross towering above you and the whole western end of Lake Ontario stretched out before you. The view is incomparable. Not only can you see all of Hamilton and its steel plants, and Burlington Bay beyond, but on the horizon you can run your eye along the whole length of the Escarpment where it parallels the lake to the north. And once again, in the misty distance to the east, if the weather's right, you can see the CN Tower and the SkyDome.

If you look straight down, you can see that the bowl has widened out into an ever-deepening, steep-sided gorge. If water's running in the creek, you should be able to see the crest of a small waterfall approximately 125 feet below you. It's worth going down to have a look. Not only is it a pretty little falls but down there you can get the clearest possible picture of how the waterfalls of the Escarpment were formed, why some of them exist in pairs, and why they have continued to flow for thousands of years.

Getting down is not as difficult as it appears from the lookout. If you're going on foot, go west on the Ridge Road till you reach the blue sign indicating a side trail of the Bruce Trail. It's only a couple of minutes' walk. An old gravel road runs down the side of the Escarpment and it's a fairly easy descent. At the bottom, at the railway tracks, you can connect with the path that takes you to the falls.

If you're driving, take a good look down before you leave. You'll see where a rail line separates the woods and the gorge from suburban Stoney Creek. If you look closely, you'll see a small parking lot on the other side of the tracks, opposite the gorge. That's where you want to end up. Pedestrians can cross the tracks there. Take the Ridge Road back to Centennial Parkway. Turn right and go down the Escarpment to King Street. Turn right again and go east on King to Mountain Avenue. Go right once more and stay on that road till you reach the railroad and the parking lot.

Once you cross the tracks you'll find it easy going. The mouth of the gorge is open-wooded and inviting. Now you can see the bowl from the bottom up.

As you approach the lower falls, you can clearly see how the ridge of rock at its crest, which is actually a layer of hard Whirlpool sandstone, has resisted erosion, while the soft red Queenston shale below it has worn away. The little waterfall has been undermined considerably. The crest, in fact, is not being worn away inch by inch but will collapse piece by piece in great blocks. The thawing and freezing of winter will be one of the forces that brings this about.

The sides of the gorge downstream are littered with these blocks. It's a fair guess that many of them weigh a ton or more. And a fair guess that they've been lying there for centuries, after falling from the crest of a waterfall.

If you turn and look upstream, you can see the upper falls in the distance. Its crest is a good 125 feet above that of the lower falls. What's happening here is the little stream is falling over two different layers of hard rock — two different kinds of rock, in fact. The upper falls is flowing over a layer of dolostone, the lower falls over a layer of sandstone.

If you turn and look at the wall of the gorge, you can see the many layers that have been cut through by erosion. The hard layers stand out prominently. It's easy to spot the dolostone at the top and the Whirlpool sandstone near the bottom. In between are thicker strata of much softer stone. Somewhere near the middle there's a third layer of hard stone, in this case, limestone.

Any one of the hard layers is resistant enough to erosion to have created a waterfall, and at times there may have been three waterfalls existing simultaneously in the short length of this gorge. There are several places on the Escarpment, even now, where waterfalls can be found in pairs, one above the other.

Finally, have a look at the two big blocks of stone that are lying in the stream bed at the crest of the lower falls. Where did they come from? Certainly not from the layer of sandstone beneath them. They almost certainly fell from some long-ago waterfall that existed well above this spot. Was it a waterfall at the level of the limestone strata or was it way up where the dolostone is? That's the kind of question that leaves a layman shaking his head. How could anyone ever know? Well, a

At the crest of the lower falls at the Devil's Punch Bowl.

geologist can have an answer for you in about five minutes. He'd mix up a 10 percent solution of hydrochloric acid, apply a bit of it to the stone in question, and if it fizzed, it would be limestone; if it didn't, it would be dolostone. Simple high school chemistry! The extraordinary thing about being able to answer that impossible question so easily is that it doesn't lessen the mysteries of this fascinating place so much as deepen them.

The gorge at DeCew Falls is a shiny sanctuary on a sunny summer afternoon.

Fifteen Mile Creek tumbles down the "steps" at Rockway Falls.

Upper Balls Falls, the prettiest of the two waterfalls on Twenty Mile Creek.

Lower Balls Falls is big and quite magnificent when it
has a full head of water.

The loveliest of waterfalls in summer, Albion Falls looks quite
forbidding in winter.

Tiffany Falls gets its name not from the famous jeweler but from Ancaster's first doctor.

Sherman Falls is a surprising discovery when you come upon it hidden in the woods.

Hundreds of people pass by little Hermitage Falls without ever knowing it's there.

Felker's Falls

On Red Hill Creek

Height – 21.5 m (70 ft)   Crest Width – 7 m (23 ft)   N 43:12:25 W 79:47:41

Felker's Falls Conservation Area

Best Time to View: Except in long periods of summer drought, Felker's usually puts on a pretty good show. It faces north and is open to the sky, though you may have to go into the gorge or over to the east rim to see it from the best angle. It's a curtain falls.

Responsible Authority:

Hamilton Region Conservation Authority, (905) 648-4427

How to Get There: Take the QEW to Exit 88 (Stoney Creek). You'll find yourself on Centennial Parkway (Hamilton-Wentworth Road 20). Go south through Stoney Creek and up the Escarpment. Continue till you reach the prosaically named Mud Street (Hamilton-Wentworth Road 411). Turn right. Go approximately 2 kilometers to Paramount Drive. Turn right. For a moment or two you'll think you've made a wrong turn and you'll find yourself wandering through a relatively new middle-class subdivision, the last place you'd expect to find a waterfall. Don't panic! You're on the right track. Follow Paramount around until you come to Ackland Street. Turn right. The conservation area and Felker's Falls are at the end of the street. There's plenty of parking.

Felker's Falls hidden in the winter shadows.

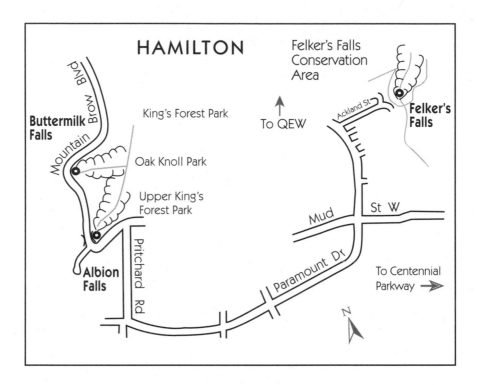

The waterfalls start to come in bunches as you near the head of the lake, and the split-rail fences proliferate as you travel deeper into the territory of the Hamilton Region Conservative Authority. The Authority is an organization with a fine touch, not only for the kind of fences it puts up but for the welcoming nature of the signs it posts. Unlike some others who have authority over parts of the Escarpment, they don't greet you with sternly worded lists of all the things you won't be allowed to do should you dare set foot on "their" property.

The trail here is dedicated to Peter Street, who did much in his short life to make the world a bit less intimidating for the disabled. Appropriately, the loop through Felker's Falls Conservation Area is wheelchair accessible, which means it's also an okay spot for people dependant on walkers or electric scooters, toddlers in strollers, and even the blind. For the less able and less experienced it's an opportunity to try out the Bruce Trail.

The path runs through a pleasant forest with a few good-sized oak and maple along the way. And it's level throughout, even where it passes the attractive Felker's Falls. The best part skirts the rim of the Escarpment above the city of Hamilton. There, you get a matchless view of Burlington Bay and the surrounding uplands. Hamiltonians, incidentally, never refer to it as the Escarpment. To them it's simply and fondly "The Mountain."

Albion Falls

On Red Hill Creek

Height – 21 m (69 ft)   Crest Width – 10 m (33 ft)   N 43:12:00 W 79:49:17

Upper King's Forest Park

Best Time to View: Most of the year, except for periods of summer drought. It's especially beautiful in late spring and early summer. It faces northeast and is open to the sky. This is a cascade with a wide, accessible ledge about two-thirds of the way down.

Responsible Authority:
  City of Hamilton, Department of Public Works & Traffic, (905) 546-2409

How to Get There: Take the QEW to Exit 88 (Stoney Creek). Follow Centennial Parkway (Hamilton-Wentworth Road 20) south through Stoney Creek and up the Escarpment. Continue till you reach Mud Street (Hamilton-Wentworth Road 411). Turn right. Go approximately 2 kilometers to Paramount Drive. Turn left. (A right turn at Paramount will take you in the direction of Felker's Falls.) Follow Paramount to Pritchard Road. Turn right. This will bring you to an older version of Mud Street, where it joins Mountain Brow Boulevard. Turn left onto Mountain Brow. It curves around the falls at this point. Park across the road in the lot at Albion Falls Park.

This is the loveliest of waterfalls. Unfortunately, it has been spoiled a little by its surroundings, principally the ugly old concrete bridge that carries Mountain Brow Boulevard over the crest of the falls. For that desecration you can blame some long-gone generation. The rusty guardrail along the edge of the gorge, however, is a more recent indignity. These things will deteriorate further and have to be replaced at some time. One hopes the people of Hamilton will then insist that Albion Falls be given a setting worthy of its beauty.

Interestingly, Red Hill Creek does a 90-degree turn to the left at the bottom of the falls, forming a natural amphitheater. You can enjoy the scene from more than a dozen locations, though climbing down the side of the gorge to get to any of these spots is somewhat difficult at the best of times and a real adventure in winter. There are stairs coming from the parking lot but they give out after a few feet.

Albion is the ancient, pre-Roman name for Britain. The falls got the name for reasons that were probably far from whimsical. William Davis was a Southern plantation owner who sided with the British in the American Revolution. He lost everything and was forced to flee, making the trek from North Carolina in 1792 with his wife, seven children, his slaves and 20 horses.

The gorge at Hamilton's Buttermilk Falls is an awesome place.

John Graves Simcoe, the Lieutenant Governor of Upper Canada, abolished slavery in 1793. That might have brought Davis into conflict with the authorities but a bitter winter tragically intervened, killing the slaves and Hannah, his beautiful Southern belle wife.

William Davis somehow persisted and may have been able to carry his loss a little more lightly after he was granted the magnificent waterfall on Red Hill Creek, along with 500 surrounding acres. Those who were able to acquire the lands atop the Escarpment were much envied. It was more lightly wooded here than elsewhere. Some farmers were even able to plow around the trees to plant their first crops.

By 1800, Davis had established Albion Mills as a thriving enterprise, so much so that he was able to build for himself one of the most ambitiously conceived homes in the colony, Harmony Hall, where he began once again to live in the grand Southern manner.

Buttermilk Falls

On Red Hill Creek

Height – 21 m (68 ft)   Crest Width – 10 m (32 ft)   N 43:12:42 W 79:49:01

Oak Knoll Park

Best Time to View: This falls is fed by a small tributary of Red Hill Creek. Only rarely does it carry enough water to produce a good show, though it can be breathtaking to peer down into the deep, round, rocky bowl, especially in midwinter. Buttermilk is a ribbon falls. It's open to the sky.

Responsible Authority:
City of Hamilton, Department of Public Works and Traffic, (905) 546-2409

How to Get There: Follow the directions for Albion Falls and then, if you're prepared to walk, take the Bruce Trail west through Upper King's Forest Park to Buttermilk. It's about a five-minute hike. If you want to drive, continue west on Mountain Brow Boulevard. In a minute or so you'll pass over the crest of the falls, though all you'll see from the car will be bridge railings. The parking lot for Oak Knoll Park is on the west side of the falls.

At one time there had to be a lot more water coming over the crest of this falls than there is now. Something had the power to scour out the great gorge. It might have been some ancient, long-lost river like the one that once flowed in the Dundas Valley or the one that created the rolling lands of Short Hills Provincial Park where Swayze Falls is located.

A mightier Red Hill Creek surely made its own contribution, before the settlers came and cut down all the trees. That changed things forever, in a fundamental way. With the trees gone the land could no longer hold water in the ground the way it once did, and streams that had been able to float fair-sized ships and barges dried up into to brooks and rivulets. Nothing will ever bring back the great forests, though the wooded areas along some parts of the Escarpment have doubled in size since the 1950s. Standing on the edge of the enormous gorge today you can only imagine what it must have looked like with a great waterfall plunging into its depths.

Chedoke Falls

On Chedoke Creek

Height – 17.5 m (57 ft)   Crest Width – 10 m (32 ft)   N 43:14:49 W 79:54:98

Mountain Face Park

Best Time to View: Being buried underground probably helps little Chedoke Creek retain water during dry periods. This waterfall shows best in the spring. It's open to the sky but the gorge is very narrow and steep. This is a ribbon falls.

Responsible Authority:
City of Hamilton, Department of Public Works and Traffic, (905) 546-2409

How to Get There: Follow Highway 403 from where it separates from the QEW and makes its way through the west end of Hamilton. It will take you up the Escarpment. Exit east onto the Lincoln Alexander Parkway then get off at the first interchange, Mohawk Road. Turn left. Follow Mohawk to Scenic Drive. Turn left again. Follow Scenic as it threads its way along the ridge of the Escarpment overlooking Hamilton. In a couple of kilometers you'll come to Colquhoun Crescent. Park your car on this street or any of the other streets nearby and walk a few meters east on Scenic till you find yourself standing on a bridge. To the south you'll see Colquhoun Park. Chedoke Creek is buried somewhere under its grassy playing fields. Go to the north side of the bridge and look over the railing. Look straight down. There, directly under your feet, you'll find the elusive Chedoke Falls.

One's instinct is to question the need to enclose this or any other waterfall with chain-link fence — Chedoke is imprisoned by it! It seems like such a heavy-handed way to treat nature. However, when you see how the sheer walls of the gorge rise above the falls to form an 80 or 90 foot drop — the equivalent of a seven- or eight-story building — you have to agree that safety comes first, especially the safety of neighborhood children.

The Bruce Trail runs along the base of the Escarpment at this point. You can get down to it by returning west half a kilometer or so, to Cliffview Park, and taking the stairs. Or you can go further east to Beckett Drive, make a left, and follow it to where it takes a sharp turn to the east. There you'll find Mountain Face Park and another set of stairs (but no place to park).

Some will think it sacrilege to say it, especially some who live in this part of Hamilton, but the stairs are a boring way to get up and down the Escarpment. First there's the tedious "clomp-clomp" of getting down and then the "Oh, my gawd, I

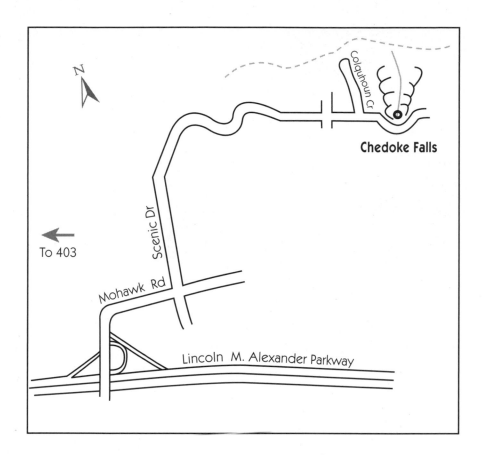

Chedoke Falls

To 403

Colquhoun Cr

Scenic Dr

Mohawk Rd

Lincoln M. Alexander Parkway

think my heart's going to give out" of getting back up again. You can drive down. Beckett Drive will take you all the way to the bottom, where a left onto Glenfern Avenue and another left onto Mountain Avenue will bring you to Hillcrest Avenue, which runs along the base of the Escarpment. You can park on this street.

Running parallel to Hillcrest is a broad track that once was the right of way for the old Chedoke Radial. Radials were a kind of heavy-duty streetcar that ran between many towns and cities in Southern Ontario in the first half of the 20th century. Alas, the automobile eventually put them out of business. They would be a pleasant way to travel today, and environmentally sensible.

The Radial Trail will take you to the mouth of the Chedoke gorge. The further west you park on Hillcrest, the closer you'll be to it. The Bruce Trail is in the woods, a little further up the base of the Escarpment. It will also take you to the gorge, though the walking is somewhat difficult in this section because the path is impregnated with stones.

Even when you've seen the gorge from above, seen how deep and narrow it is, it's a shock to encounter it from below. It's one of the wildest, most out-of-this-

Huge blocks of caprock line the stream below Chedoke Falls.

world places on the Escarpment — and here it is, hidden away in a spot close to the geographical center of one of Canada's largest cities!

Chedoke Creek goes underground again at the mouth of the gorge, leaving an open stretch of only 300 meters or so between that point and the falls. Normally you could walk that distance in three or four minutes. Not here! Walking in any normal sense is impossible. You might reach the falls by climbing partway up the side of the gorge and working your along, but it's difficult and dangerous. If you don't lose your perch somehow and take a precipitous tumble, you'll still be in danger of setting off a landslide in the loose, heavy shale.

The banks of the creek are piled high with enormous blocks of caprock. The sides of the gorge are so steep and so unstable it appears that anything that has fallen from above, even pieces weighing several tons, has slid all the way to the bottom. Only by climbing over these rocks can you reach the falls with any assurance of safety. If you're in reasonable shape, you can do it. You'll enjoy the challenge. It's a wild and improbable journey in the midst of a land of steel mills, shopping malls and sprawling suburbs. Count on spending an hour or two at it. Take a lunch. You'll be delighted to discover a couple of smaller waterfalls along the way.

Tiffany Falls

On Tiffany Creek

LOWER FALLS
Height – 19 m (58.5 ft)   Crest Width – 8 m (26 ft)   N 43:14:55 W 79:57:62

UPPER FALLS
Height – 6.5 m (21 ft)   Crest Width – 7 m (23 ft)

Tiffany Falls Conservation Area

Best Time to View: Spring and fall. When Tiffany Creek is full, these are two of the prettiest waterfalls imaginable. The lower falls is open to the sky but the deep, narrow gorge will often put it in shadow. The upper falls is under forest cover. Both are cascades.

Responsible Authority:
Hamilton Region Conservation Authority, (905) 648-4427

How to Get There: Follow Highway 403 from where it separates from the QEW and makes its way through the west end of Hamilton. It will take you up the Escarpment. Exit at Mohawk Road and follow it west through one of those lovely neighborhoods that make Ancaster such an envied community. Along the way, Mohawk will change its name to Rousseaux, but don't let that throw you off. At Wilson Street, the main street of Ancaster, turn right. You'll now be heading back down the Escarpment in a long, gentle descent. Keep your eyes open for a pull-off area on the right. It's about 2 kilometers from where you made the turn. There should be a sign to tell you that you've found Tiffany Falls Conservation Area and parking for several cars. The falls are about a five-minute hike up the gorge.

We made the short trek in from the road early one Sunday morning. Overhead we had one of those baby blue winter skies. Underfoot we had 25 centimeters of fresh powder snow. Even the sting of the cold in our faces was a welcome sensation.

It takes only a few minutes to reach the falls, but the steep walls of the gorge are unstable in spots and the going can be awkward and difficult. In wet weather it can be downright dangerous. We were thankful to some early riser for breaking trail and showing us the surest route.

We both lost our footing and tumbled into the snow several times. It was nothing. There wasn't a chance of getting hurt. It was like eiderdown, it was so soft. We paused once to catch our breath and to appreciate the surroundings. Everything was so clean and bright. The silence was surreal.

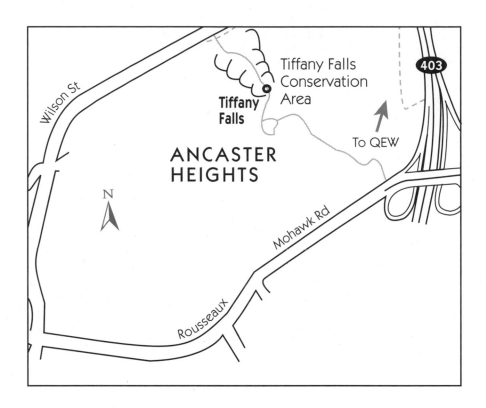

We expected to hear the sound of falling water long before we did, and when we did it was faint and had no presence. When we got to the head of the gorge, Tiffany Falls was barely discernable in the deep, wintery shadows. It was completely frozen over. It towered above us some four or five stories high, looking like a colossal pipe organ that had been fashioned out of polished glass. Somewhere in its interior the water continued to flow. We could hear it dripping rhythmically, measuring time as faithfully as a clock.

The tracks of the early riser led up the side of the gorge to the left of the falls and disappeared at the edge of the sky. We made no attempt to follow. It would be a couple of months before we would take that same route and discover another Tiffany Falls hidden in the woods beyond.

Mill Falls

On Ancaster Creek

Height – 9 m (30 ft)　　　Crest Width – 4.5 m (15 ft)　　　N 43:13:07　W 79:58: 54

Ancaster Mountain Mill

Best Time to View: Ancaster Creek seems to hold its water levels pretty well for a small stream, and for most of the year this series of small ribbon falls puts on a romantic show for diners in the restaurant at the mill. The waterfalls face north and are partly open to the sky.

Responsible Authority: Old Mill Restaurant, (905) 648-1827

How to Get There: Follow Highway 403 from where it separates from the QEW and makes its way through the west end of Hamilton. It will take you up the Escarpment. Exit at Mohawk Road and go west. Along the way it'll change its name to Rousseaux, but don't let that throw you off. When you come to Wilson Street, turn right. You'll find yourself going back down the Escarpment. Keep an eye to your left for Montgomery Drive, which is less than a kilometer away. At Montgomery, turn left. Almost immediately you'll find yourself at Old Dundas Road. Turn left again. Travel another short distance till you come to the Ancaster Mountain Mill. There's plenty of parking both above and below the mill. The waterfalls are behind the building.

This is a lovely place to be almost any day of the year, though if you were to choose a perfect time, it would probably be some fresh summer Sunday morning. The restaurant spans the water and lines both sides of the stream. Some diners sit suspended 20 feet above the rushing waters. A privileged few sit outside, so close to one of the little waterfalls they can reach out and touch the water.

The mill towers over the busy little stream and easily dominates the soft features of the surrounding glen. It's a fine building, a tribute to the stonemason's craft, but it's not the original mill on Ancaster Creek. This one was built in 1863. There were four others before it, not all of them on the same site. In the space of 70 years, all were destroyed by fire.

It's not the waterfalls or the mills that make this particular spot on the Escarpment so fascinating; it's the people who settled here. Anyone looking for material for a great Canadian historical novel is sure to find it in and around Ancaster. There's plenty enough for a string of sequels as well.

This is a beautiful place and always has been. One English traveler who passed through in the early days wrote that, even though it was still wild and unsettled, it was "perhaps as beautiful and romantic as any in the interior of America." An exceptional landscape, not unexpectedly, often attracts exceptional people.

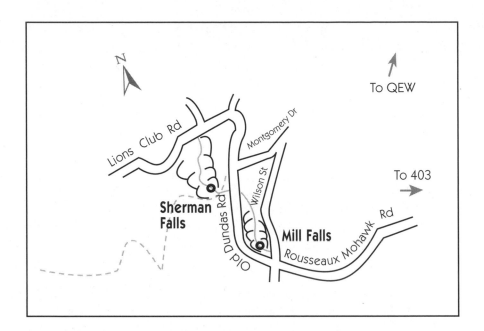

There was Jean Baptiste Rousseaux. He, his father and his grandfather were interpreters. As such they were witness to many of the treaties the British negotiated with the First Nations People. Rousseaux bought the mill in 1794. Everybody called him St. John, and Ancaster, in fact, was at one time known as St. John's Mill. Rousseaux married Margaret Clyne, who was brought up by Joseph Brant after most of her family was killed by hostile natives.

There was Richard Beasley who, like Rousseaux, first came to the area as a fur trader. Beasley may have been the first to settle at the head of the lake. He certainly was its first true entrepreneur. He not only built the original mill, in partnership with James Wilson, but he amassed some 13,000 acres of land, 1,000 of them on his own estate below the Escarpment on Burlington Heights. In 1791 he married Henrietta Springer, whom he found wandering in tears on the shores of Cootes Paradise. She had just escaped from a band of natives who had kidnapped her. Her mother was one of the many widows who came to Canada as a United Empire Loyalist, and Henrietta was one of nine children. She and Beasley had eight children.

Then there was Augustus Jones, the colorful Welshman who was deputy provincial surveyor. He laid out much of the surrounding land and gave us the grid of streets and roads we are familiar with today. Twice he married native women and was as much assimilated by native culture as his good friend Joseph Brant was by European culture.

Brant, though he lived on the other side of Burlington Bay, was often in the area. It was in a tavern owned by Beasley that he accidentally stabbed his own son with a dagger while trying to get him to leave. It was just a superficial wound but the young man died of blood poisoning. That sent Brant into a paroxysm of despair and he soon followed his son to the grave.

There were a host of others whose lives were almost as colorful: the Hatt brothers, who were among the founders of both Ancaster and Dundas; Oliver Tiffany, the town's first physician, for whom Tiffany Falls is named; Sir Allan Napier McNabb, the boy hero of the War of 1812 and the man who saved Canada for its British masters in the Rebellion of 1837. He became a railroad baron, premier of Ontario, and the laird of Dundurn Castle.

The most incredible story of all, one that reads like a movie script, was that of Robert Land. He had a price on his head for aiding the British during the American Revolution. A friend, a Quaker named Ralph Morden, helped him escape and paid for it with his own life. He was hanged by the American patriots.

Land fled north to Upper Canada, losing contact with his wife, Phoebe, and their seven children in the process. He crossed to Niagara in 1784 where, as a Loyalist, he was granted 200 acres just above Horseshoe Falls, on land that later became famous as the site of the Battle of Lundy's Lane. There he settled into deep depression. He obviously felt responsible for Ralph Morden's death and feared his family was lost to him forever. The incessant roar of the falls played on his nerves till he couldn't stand it any longer. He abandoned the property and wandered off into the wilderness. When he reached Burlington Bay he stopped and built himself a lean-to cabin on the deserted shore. There he settled into solitude and began to live the life a of a hermit.

Meanwhile, in 1789, Phoebe Land and the children made their own way to Niagara. There by chance they met a trader who told them about a man matching Robert's description who was living alone at the head of the lake. Phoebe and some of her older children set out to find him. In what could be the moving, tearful scene at the end of the movie, Phoebe and the children walked into the clearing where Robert was huddled over a fire in front of the lean-to, puffing silently on his pipe. The Land family was, in fact, the founding family of Hamilton and that story has been handed down from generation to generation.

It doesn't end there. It's said that Robert Land encouraged Anne, Ralph Morden's widow, to bring her own large family to the head of the lake. They were given Loyalist grants of 1,700 acres where Dundas now stands and built the first mill on Spencer Creek. Dundas was originally called Morden's Mills.

And there's just one more twist: Robert Land was the great-great-great-grandfather of Charles Lindbergh! This story and much of the information about the others comes from Marjorie Freeman Campbell's fine history of Hamilton, *A Mountain and a City*.

The Ancaster of today is as pretty as any town could hope to be. Its citizens have somehow been able to retain its integrity as one of Ontario's most historic towns without suppressing the energy needed to be a vital part of Hamilton-Wentworth. It's hard then to believe that one of the most brutish acts in Canadian history took place here, during the War of 1812 — the Ancaster Bloody Assizes.

Ancaster's Old Mill Restaurant "embraces" tiny Mill Falls.

At the time of the war, a large percentage of the people in Upper Canada were Americans. They had crossed the border after the Revolution to settle on what people in another era called the "Fat Lands of Ontario." It was the nearest good land available on the American frontier. A large number of them believed the time would soon come when Upper Canada would be part of the United States. With the War of 1812 many thought the time was at hand and openly consorted with the enemy.

(In some respects treason wasn't viewed as the unmitigated evil that it is now. In 1812 the British were at war with the French as well as the Americans, yet Napoleon was able to place an order in London for 50,000 greatcoats. While Englishmen were dying for their country, their mothers, wives and daughters were home furiously cutting and stitching for the enemy.)

The authorities in Upper Canada were determined to make an example of some of the high-handed Americans in their midst. In 1814 they charged 19 men with treason. Fifteen of them were convicted and eight were sentenced to be drawn and quartered on Burlington Heights.

Squire Richard Beasley was beside himself that all this should have taken place in his jurisdiction, and that he should have been compelled to be a part of it. He had long wanted to be an important man and he had succeeded. Among other things, he was a justice of the peace in Ancaster. As such he was one of those charged with arresting the men, confiscating their property, keeping them locked in the lower confines of the mill while the trial was on, and marching them down the Escarpment to their deaths when it was over.

People then weren't squeamish about cruel punishments. Floggings and hangings were public events. But to hang men and cut them down while they were still alive and then rip their guts open and dismember them....

It was the last time that dreaded sentence was carried out in the British Empire. They say it so sickened poor Beasley that he never got over it.

It's not likely the Sunday-morning diners give much thought to such things, not when they have the sun, the soft sound of falling water and carpets of forget-me-nots along the banks of the creek to go with their coffee and croissants.

Sherman Falls

On Ancaster Creek

Height – 12 m (39 ft)   Crest Width – 7 m (23 ft)   N 43:14:49 W 79:58:35

Private Property

Best Time to View: Nothing seems able to diminish the beauty of Sherman Falls, not the lower water levels of midsummer or the buildup of ice in midwinter. It's a steep cascade with a wide, accessible ledge about two-thirds of the way down. It faces north and is shaded by forest cover.

How to Get There: Follow Highway 403 from where it separates from the QEW and makes its way through the west end of Hamilton. It will take you up the Escarpment. Exit at Mohawk Road and go west. Along the way it will become Rousseaux; keep going. At Wilson Street turn right. You'll now find yourself heading back down the Escarpment. Keep an eye open to your left for Montgomery Drive, which is less than a kilometer away. Turn left. Almost immediately you'll find yourself at the Old Dundas Road. Turn right. This will take you further down the Escarpment. Very soon you'll come to a bridge where Old Dundas Road intersects with Lions Club Road. The falls is in the woods to your left. The only sign you're likely to see is one for the Bruce Trail. Park on Lions Club Road on the side nearest the woods.

We arrived at Sherman Falls one bright morning to find a beam of sunlight streaming through the trees, illuminating a big rock in the shadows at the water's edge. With the falls looming majestic in the background, it promised to be a dramatic photograph. Alas, by the time we unlimbered the camera gear, the sun was gone and so was the potential for a great picture. Mikal was convinced, however, that the light would return and that it would strike the rock in the same way again. He hunkered down behind the camera to wait.

Not me! Not yet! Sherman Falls is a sudden sanctuary in the midst of a whirling megalopolis. After you do the requisite dance of death with the 18-wheelers on the 401 and the QEW to get to this place, it takes a few minutes to throttle back your nervous system and readjust your psyche to nature's more benign presence.

There's a small, sturdy bridge over the creek about 50 meters or so below the falls. I crossed it and worked my way up the gorge on the other side to the watery ledge that divides the upper part of the falls from the lower. There I stood, at arm's length from the falling water, the sound of it enveloping me completely, wondering if there could possibly be anything on the Escarpment more inviting, more revivifying than this. (Having visited some three dozen others since then, the answer is no.)

Sherman Falls
in perpetual
shadow.

Sherman is not a small waterfall. It's a good three or four stories high. But because it's in the woods at the head of this narrow, almost secret little gorge, and because you can safely climb right up onto it, it seems smaller and more intimate.

I had a notion to take my shoes and socks off and wade across the falls to the other side. I didn't and later wished I had. There are some impulses we should always give in to, even in middle age — perhaps especially in middle age.

Eventually, I climbed back down and joined Mikal in his wait for the sun. As we sat there, a young woman came along the path on the other side of the stream. Without so much as a glance in our direction she bent down and dipped her face in the cold water. We watched as she then climbed up the slope to the ledge and sat on the same rock as I had. She was quite still for several minutes. I watched her, thinking about the need many of us have to go off on our own occasionally and spend time with nobody but ourselves. I wondered, too, if a young woman alone could be safe here, at least as safe as she would be on the nearby city streets. I hoped the answer was yes.

She broke her reverie — and mine — by taking off her shoes and splashing about in the water. From where we sat, looking up at her and not being able to see the surface of the ledge, it looked like she was dancing on air. Then suddenly she turned and without hesitation walked right into the waterfall, clothes and all. She bravely stood there for several long moments, immersed in the chilly water. Like I said, there are some impulses we should always give in to.

In a few minutes she came down the path, shoes in hand, shaking her long hair like a happy spaniel.

"That was a wonderful, crazy thing to do," we told her.

"I only found out about this place last year," she replied, "though I've lived around here all my life. I love that waterfall."

With that she smiled and was gone. We turned back to the camera. The sun had broken through the trees and once again it was shining on the big rock, just as Mikal had assured me it would.

Hermitage Falls

On Hermitage Creek

Height – 3.5 m (12 ft)   Crest Width – 2.5 m (8 ft)   N 43:14:56   W 79:59:46

Dundas Valley Conservation Area

Best Time to View: It's a small waterfall fed by a small stream, but a stream that drains a relatively large area, making it a reliable source of water most of the year. Hermitage is a cascade facing north and it's in shade.

Responsible Authority:
Hamilton Region Conservation Authority, (905) 648-4427

How to Get There: Follow Highway 403 from where it separates from the QEW and makes its way through the west end of Hamilton. It will take you up the Escarpment. Exit at Mohawk Road and go west. Along the way it will become

Hermitage Falls.

Rousseaux; carry on down the road. At Wilson, the main street of Ancaster, turn left and go to Sulphur Springs Road. Turn right. Now you'll find yourself on one of the loveliest roads in Southern Ontario. Take your time and enjoy it. A couple of kilometers along, on your right, you'll see a sign for the Hermitage, one of the many properties in the Dundas Valley owned or controlled by the Hamilton Region Conservation Authority. Pull into the parking lot and walk back to the entrance. Surprise! The waterfall is hidden in the trees on the east side of the driveway.

Below the falls, Hermitage Creek flows around an old gatehouse and then encounters a second drop, which is more of a waterslide than a waterfall or a rapid. The little creek negotiates this obstacle without a flicker of whitewater.

The trail here is one of the most popular in the valley. It leads to the ruins of an old mansion, the Hermitage, which burned many years ago.

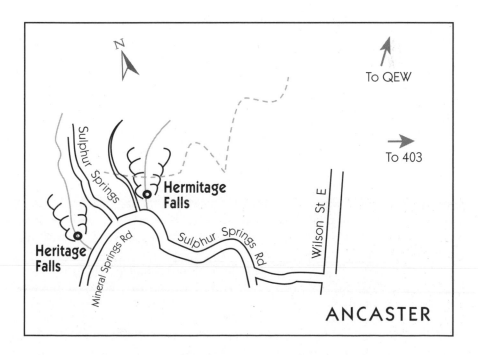

Heritage Falls

Branch of Sulphur Creek

Height – 3.5 m (12 ft)   Crest Width – 2.5 m (8 ft)   N 43:14:54   W 79:59:82

Dundas Valley Conservation Area

Best Time to View: This is a small waterfall fed by a small stream that drains a very limited area, so it is almost certain to be dry from late spring to late fall. It's a ribbon falls that faces north and is heavily shaded.

Responsible Authority:

Hamilton Region Conservation Authority, (905) 648-4427

How to Get There: Follow Highway 403 from where it separates from the QEW and makes its way through the west end of Hamilton. It will take you up the Escarpment. Exit at Mohawk Road and go west. Along the way it will become Rousseaux; don't let that throw you off. Turn left at Wilson Street and go to Sulphur Springs Road. Turn right. Follow this for about 2 kilometers until you come to a split in the road where Sulphur Springs takes a sharp turn to the north. Keep going straight! You are now on Mineral Springs Road. It's just past this point, on your right, that you'll find the Griffin House. You'll have to keep a sharp eye open for it. The sign at the bottom of the lane isn't easy to see. The falls is about a 10-minute walk north of the house.

The faint remains of an old cart-track drew us up the slight rise from Mineral Springs Road to Griffin House, which stands in silent dignity, deep in the shade of spruce and maple.

As ancestral homes go, the house is as modest as modest can be, with just two rooms on the main floor, a kitchen and a parlor, and a couple of bedrooms upstairs, tucked away under the eaves.

We pressed our faces to the kitchen window. Inside everything looked so austere and yet so real. It was as if Enerals and Pricilla Griffin had merely gone for a walk and their return would bring the house back to life again. Their homestead had not suffered the fate of being fancified and prettified like so many museum-piece pioneer homes.

Like most people of their time, the Griffins almost certainly lived simple lives, lives consumed by hard work. Unlike so many of us, they were bound to be comfortable and secure in the knowledge that the long river of time would eventually take them to eternity. That doesn't mean theirs was joyless existence. David Martin, a Scottish shepherd who was a contemporary of the Griffins, lived in the great Beverley Swamp, far to the other side of the Dundas Valley. He was able to capture the spirit and tempo of those times in a bit of verse.

In the rough old time and the tough old times
Full thirty years ago,
There was not a clock in the settlement
To tell how the time did go;
But we knew very well when the day began,
And we knew very well when 'twas o'er.
And our dinner bell was the gude wife's shout
When the sun reached the nick in the door.

Back of the house the land falls away gently, and we could see across the valley for some distance to the north. A stout old shed stood some ways down the slope. It had managed to resist heaving and leaning despite the weight of its years. Now it was in the process of being smothered by vines that had all but overgrown it. Not far away stood an ancient apple tree, half of it naked and dead, the other half so loaded with fruit it was barely able to hold its branches off the ground.

It was a lovely walk, with the afternoon heat drawing forth all the smells of summer. The Conservation Authority had cut a broad, grassy path through what had become a much overgrown meadow. It almost certainly would have been pasture or cropland when the Griffin family farmed it.

Milkweed lined the way. Patches of Queen Anne's lace were everywhere the sun shone hardest. The goldenrod was "ripening." Soon its feathery crowns of mustard yellow would transform the landscape for the last phase of summer. On all sides we saw a land in transition. Clumps of bushes, alders mostly, had already driven away everything within their shadows, and here and there saplings were beginning to reach for the sky. Not many years from now it will cease to be a meadow and become a young forest. In a generation, the walk to little Heritage Falls will be through a shadowy woods.

We were not surprised to find the little waterfall dry. The stream is just a little riffle of a thing that drains an area not much bigger than the farm itself. Still, it wasn't difficult for us to imagine how complete the scene would be when the water flowed again. The creek runs through a sunny area of marsh before it passes under the path and makes its way through a stand of slim, graceful trees. It then tumbles over the falls into a small wooded glen that is as intimate as your living room. It was only midsummer but the path was already littered with walnuts.

You can almost feel the presence of the Griffins. Surely they came here often, perhaps in the evenings when the chores were done. To them it would have been the Promised Land after their perilous flight from slavery 165 years ago. What were their thoughts when they visited this place? Did the land look more beautiful because it was theirs to own and cherish?

On our return we encountered a huge oak that had to be at least 200 years old, old enough to have outlived eight or ten generations of humans, old enough to have been silent witness to all that had ever gone on at the Griffin Homestead. It lifted not a leaf to us as we passed.

Webster's Falls

On Spencer Creek

Height – 21 m (69 ft)   Crest Width – 24 m (78 ft)   N 43:16:80 W 79:58:90

Spencer Gorge Wilderness Area
Webster's Falls Park

Best Time to View: In spring, when the water is high, this spectacular curtain falls is a miniature Niagara. In summer, when the flow diminishes, it alters character but is no less spectacular. It faces east and is open to the sky.

Responsible Authority:
Hamilton Region Conservation Authority, (905) 648-4427

How to Get There: Follow Highway 403 from where it separates from the QEW and makes its way through the west end of Hamilton. Exit at Main Street and go west. Main will change to Osler Drive and then back to Main Street again. Keep on going. You'll soon come to King Street in Dundas. Turn left. As you drive through town, keep an eye open on your right for Sydenham Road (Hamilton-Wentworth Road 505). Turn right. This will take you up the Escarpment. Keep going till Sydenham Road makes a sharp turn to the right. Don't make the turn! Keep going straight a few meters to Harvest Road. Turn left. Stay on this road for about 2.5 kilometers. Keep an eye open for Short Road. Turn left. This will take you to Webster's Falls, though there's no sign at the turn to indicate that you're on the right track. Soon a sharp turn to the left will bring you onto Fallsview Road, which will take you right into the parking lot. Expect to pay an entrance fee in season.

Nearby Tews Falls is higher by 20 meters but Webster's Falls is the bigger attraction. Far more water spills over its brink and it's much more accessible.

You can view it nicely from both sides and from virtually every angle. You can walk out on a ledge of caprock at the crest and turn and almost face the water as it goes sliding over the brink. You can take a flight of stairs all the way to the bottom of the gorge and connect with a path that brings you right to the base of the falls. And, except when water levels are very high, you can set your tripod up in the middle of the stream and take spectacular pictures as the water comes thundering down at you.

You'll find the ubiquitous blocks of capstone here, big ones, lying in the stream bed. These are particularly well placed. People can't resist pulling themselves up onto them, to enjoy the view, to dig into a lunch bag, to read a book, or to pop the big question.

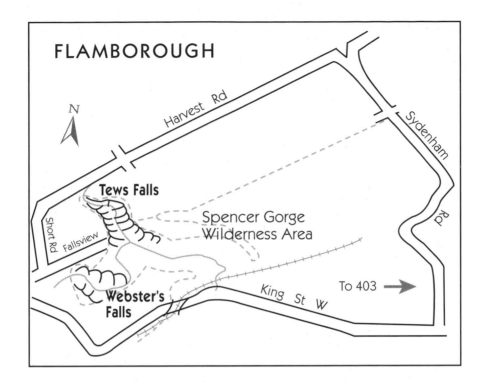

FLAMBOROUGH

N

Harvest Rd

Sydenham Rd

Tews Falls

Short Rd

Fallsview

Spencer Gorge
Wilderness Area

Webster's
Falls

King St W

To 403 →

From the moment Europeans first set eyes on it, this waterfall must have been viewed as a prized possession. Ownership changed hands a number of times in the quarter century before the Webster family claimed it in 1819. It was variously called Flamborough Falls, Spencer's Falls, Fisher's Falls, and Hatt's Falls. Joseph Webster bought it along with 127 acres of land, most of it in the gorge below, from Sheriff Titus Simons. It had been owned by Hector Sutherand Mackay, but he had lost it to the taxman.

Webster later bought more and better land around the falls, for this is where he and his family were determined to make a new life for themselves, perhaps even to become part of the New World aristocracy that Lieutenant Governor John Graves Simcoe had talked about 25 years before. There were plenty of men and women around who could qualify. Four of General Brock's brothers, for example, had taken up 700 acres of land above the Escarpment in Flamborough Township.

Upstream on Spencer Creek, James Crooks, who came from Kilmarnock in Scotland, was busy developing Crooks' Hollow. In the War of 1812 he was one of those who charged onto the field after Brock was killed and captured the invading Americans. The name Crooks' Hollow may have a bucolic ring to it, but between 1820 and 1850, James Crooks made it into what may well have been the most heavily industrialized spot in Upper Canada. He had a sawmill; an oat and barley mill; a distillery; a linseed-oil mill; a clothing mill; a rake, hoe and scythe factory; a foundry; a tannery; a cooperage; a blacksmith's shop; an ox-shoeing stall and a general store. In 1826 he began operating the first paper mill in Ontario. You can still see the ruins of some of these enterprises if you follow Harvest Road west to the other side of Brock Road, into the little community still known as Crooks' Hollow.

One neighbor the Websters probably didn't take to easily was an opinionated little Scot who would one day rise to become the rapscallion of Upper Canada politics. William Lyon Mackenzie arrived in the colony a year after the Websters and ran a drugstore-cum-bookstore on the north bank of Spencer Creek, well below Webster's Falls.

Joseph Webster himself was a half-pay army officer from Gloucester. (The rocky face of the Escarpment would certainly have reminded him of the Cotswolds.) He was one of the many thousands made idle by the end of the Napoleonic Wars, though it doesn't appear that he was as financially embarrassed as were many of his fellow officers. After all, the waterfall and the surrounding land must have commanded a handsome sum.

And the Websters must have had hopes of becoming prosperous. The industrial age was dawning. While steamboats were still timid about venturing onto the oceans, there were already three of them afloat on Lake Ontario. The family may well have seen one of them on their way to the head of the lake. Dundas was the most important community between York (Toronto) and the American border. The five most important roads started or stopped here, including the famous Dundas Street, which is still in evidence in towns and cities from Toronto to London. The family had acquired a major waterfall on a substantial stream. In the course of just 12 miles, Spencer Creek dropped 615 feet, including the plunge over Webster's Falls. That was a lot of waterpower to attract the fledgling industries of a growing colony. And people of means were quick to take advantage of it. Soon there were 20 mills in and around the town. (The Mississauga natives, incidentally, called Spencer Creek "Etobicoke," which was their word for the black alder.)

There's little to tell about the Webster's early years. Presumably they busied themselves as most pioneer families did, ridding the land of the indomitable forest so that it could be farmed and made prosperous. Unlike so many others, they seem to have resisted the temptation to cut down everything in sight.

There's a nice little stone wall running along the bank of the creek, just above the falls. It's a good place to sit and study the trees. Behind you, you'll find a very old beech, a magnificent tree. Behind that there are several gigantic oaks growing on the slope and along the path that leads to the meadow above the falls. In front of you, in the parkland across the water, there are more big trees — cedar, oak, maple and especially willow. One of the largest willows you'll ever see stands near the stone bridge. It's a guess, but most of the trees appear to be 200 years old or older, which means they were here when the Websters arrived. In the 100 years that they lived near the waterfall, the family would have watched them grow into giants. If only trees could talk.

Stairs descend into the gorge at Webster's Falls.

In 1832, Joseph Webster II, who was 10 years old when the family arrived from England, rebuilt a small distillery into Ashbourne Industries, a mill that became one of the largest industrial enterprises in the colony.

In 1848, in a spectacular bit of engineering, he built the road that takes you up the Escarpment on the west side of Dundas. (It has long been part of Highway 8, or what was formerly Highway 8. The provincial government has recently turned many of the older highways over to local authorities.) As you reach the top of this road, just before it curves to the north to go through Greensville, you are treated to an incomparable view of the Dundas Valley.

About that same time, the younger Webster also built the family's big manor house, which still stands on Webster's Falls Road. The road connects with Highway 8 but is closed to traffic. It can be reached on foot, from the park. We don't know how wealthy the family became, but tax records confirm that they were among the largest contributors to the public coffers. Joseph Webster III was prominent in his own right. He developed the family farm into a showplace of orchards and vineyards.

Joseph Webster senior, alas, got to see and appreciate none of this. About the time the mill was being readied for operation, he was on his way back to England for a visit. He and his ship disappeared without a trace somewhere on the North Atlantic.

There's a little knoll on the edge of the gorge, just north of the parking lot. It was the family's burial ground. It's overgrown now with sumac and there's the base of a broken headstone in the middle of the path. There must have been something special about it, for the family to chose this spot to bury their dead. Perhaps they found it a solemn place to end a summer's day, watching a hawk circle the darkening gorge, listening to the sounds of approaching night.

The headstones have been collected and incorporated into a memorial at the base of the knoll, where the Bruce Trail enters the woods to go north to Tews Falls. Joseph II and his wife, Maria, are represented, but Joseph III, who lived to be 91 and died in 1923, is buried in the cemetery of Christ Church, a beautiful building you can walk to through Webster's Falls Road. It's on Highway 8 just west of where it separates from Brock Road.

After the death of Joseph II in 1886, the Ashbourne Mill was sold to George Harper and W. S. Merrill. It burned in 1898, on the very day that Canadians were celebrating the 31st anniversary of Confederation. Harper then organized the Harper Electric Light and Power Company and built a powerhouse on the site of the mill. It supplied electricity to the town of Dundas, though not for long. The powerhouse burned two years later and was never replaced. The stairs down the side of the gorge are all that remain. Two disastrous fires in two years ruined George Harper and he left the area.

As late as the 1980s some people were proposing to build a new power plant at the falls. The citizens of Dundas would have none of it. Not at their waterfall! And it was and is their waterfall and has been for along time.

After the First World War, Webster's Falls passed into the hands of Lt. Col. W. E. S. Knowles, "Wesky" as the local people liked to call him. When he died in 1931 he left the falls and the surrounding land to the citizens of Dundas, plus $235,000 in trust to maintain it as a park. It was not until recently that the place was anything but a pleasure to them. That's when they were told that the park's beautiful old stone bridge had been declared a historic site and under provincial regulations would cost a fortune to restore and make safe. Worse still, Colonel Knowles' generous bequest had been reduced to a relative pittance by inflation. Hence the proposal to build a new hydroelectric generating plant to help defray costs.

When you leave to drive back down to Dundas, head left instead of right when you reach Harvest Road. That will take you to Brock Road, which is a short distance away. Turn left and follow this to where it joins with Highway 8 and takes you to the lookout on the edge of the Escarpment and that magnificent view of the Dundas Valley. As you stand there, taking it all in, try to imagine the long-gone ancient river called Erigan that once flowed through here. Imagine too, if you can, a great canal running down the middle of this valley, taking ships from Lake Erie to Lake Ontario. The Government of Upper Canada actually started work on such a canal. It was to run from the mouth of the Grand River to Burlington Bay. They abandoned the project because they said there simply wasn't enough money in the colony to see it through. The Welland Canal was built instead. By 1867 the government had, in fact, spent $7,638,240 building and rebuilding it, far more than it said it couldn't afford to spend on the original canal project. What a sight it would be now to stand high on the Escarpment and watch enormous lake freighters and great ocean-going vessels sail down the middle of the Dundas Valley.

Tews Falls

On Logie's Creek

Height – 41 m (134 ft)   Crest Width – 10 m (32 ft)   N 43:16:92W 79:58:72

Spencer Gorge Wilderness Area

Best Time to View: This can be a magnificent waterfall but only when there's enough water in little Logie's Creek to put on a good show. Early spring is obviously the best time, though Tews can be dazzling in late winter with the spectacular buildup of ice at its base. This is a ribbon falls facing southeast, open to the sky.

Responsible Authority:

Hamilton Region Conservation Authority, (905) 648-4427

How to Get There: Follow Highway 403 from where it separates from the QEW and makes its way through the west end of Hamilton. Exit at Main Street and go west; it will change to Osler Drive and then back again to Main Street. Keep going! You'll soon come to King Street in Dundas. Turn left. As you drive through town, keep an eye to the right for Sydenham Road (Hamilton-Wentworth Road 505). Turn right. This will take you up the Escarpment. Keep going till Sydenham Road makes a sharp turn to the right. Don't make the turn! Keep going straight a few meters to Harvest Road and turn left. Stay on this road for about 2 kilometers till you come to an old railway underpass. The parking lot for Tews Falls is just west of this. Expect to pay an entry fee in season. There's no sign to indicate that it's wheelchair or stroller accessible, but the path leading to the lower of the two viewing platforms is fairly level and the going is relatively easy. The falls is approximately 100 meters from the parking lot.

We bounded out of the car on one of those peerless spring mornings and, without even pausing to get our bearings, headed immediately for the woods at the back of the long meadow that stretches south from the parking lot. The only other water-fall we knew at that time was Webster's. We weren't expecting Tews and many of the other waterfalls of the Escarpment to be so close to the road. We just assumed they would be a bit beyond easy reach. (We weren't expecting Webster's to be so close to Tews, either. On foot it's just the other side of that woods at the back of the meadow.)

It wasn't a mistake to regret. The grass in the meadow was still only ankle deep and still a rich spring green. Best of all, the land had that earthy smell again.

We got almost to the edge of the woods before we were able to hear the falls. It was somewhere behind us! We circled back, walking along the split-rail fence that borders the gorge. What a place for a picnic! What a spot to settle down and break out the muffins and the coffee Thermos! Why hadn't we thought of it?

Soon we were able to see Logie's Creek through the still-leafless trees. The sun danced shyly across the water where it was poised to spill over the brink. It's a demure little stream. We expected to find a demure little waterfall to match. We couldn't have been more wrong.

It took us a couple of minutes to work our way around to the other side, passing a bog that was bright with marsh marigolds and crossing over a small wooden bridge. Then we were taken completely by surprise. Though it doesn't have much water in it, Tews is an awesome waterfall nevertheless. It plunges deep into the gorge from a height that is almost equal that of Niagara. (Geologists have calculated that many centuries ago it actually was higher, when Tews was 200 meters further downstream.) Though it doesn't have Niagara's volume — we're talking about the waters of Logie's Creek versus four of the Great Lakes — it does have some of the same power to mesmerize as you watch the water slip effortlessly over the edge and fall ever so slowly in long, twisting veils. It's a full moment and more before it splashes into the pool below.

We climbed the stairs to the upper viewing platform, realizing as we went that it would be a difficult waterfall to observe if the Hamilton Region Conservation Authority hadn't sited both platforms well out on the edge of the gorge. (They were originally constructed entirely of wood, but the railings were replaced with metal frames after some people of questionable sanity stole a brand new Jeep Cherokee from a local dealership and pushed it off the lower platform into the gorge.)

A path from the upper platform took us along the edge of the Spencer Gorge Wilderness Area to Dundas Peak. We discovered it wasn't a peak in any sense of it being a mountain but a high, rocky headland from which you can see the town of Dundas at your feet and all of Hamilton and Burlington Bay in the distance. It's not a long walk, but it took us 10 or 15 minutes to get there. With spring bursting out all around us we weren't in any hurry.

The beech trees looked ready to blossom and the mayapples, with their exquisite white flowers, were everywhere underfoot. Off in the gorge one could hear the unmistakable sounds of blue jays and cardinals. That wasn't all. Mikal, with his far more acute hearing and eyesight and his infinitely greater knowledge of things in the wild, drew my attention to turkey vultures flying high overhead and, much closer to hand, a catbird and a flycatcher, all recently returned from wintering in the south.

Though it was midweek, we were far from alone. The path to the Dundas Peak, we soon learned, is a favorite walking place for people from miles around.

We visited Tews many times after that. It became one of our favorite spots on the Escarpment. In some ways we liked it even better in winter. Then we would often find the falls in a solemn, misty mood, the water having lost its summer luster and taken on shades of ochre. Then it fell into the gorge in an almost leaden manner. At the bottom of the bowl there would be a huge ice dome and spiraling

A winter morning at Tews Falls near Dundas.

ice castles rising up to meet the falling water. All around, the rock walls would be cloaked in ice that had a mysterious blue tinge to it, giving it a kind of inner light that we had once associated only with icebergs and glaciers.

On one snapping cold day, we found deer tracks in the snow at the very edge of the gorge. Another short step and the animal would have plunged to its death on the rocks below. Are they that surefooted or do they take stupid chances like humans and sometimes lose their lives? A fall at Tews would be the equivalent of plummeting from an 11-story building.

Surprisingly, it took several visits before we discovered that we could easily walk from Tews to Webster's and back again in a matter of minutes. The drive from one to the other takes you a very long way around. We soon found ourselves wishing the walk were equally long. In all of Southern Ontario there isn't a more splendid-looking place than the Spencer Gorge. A walk along its wooded rim at any time of the year, in any weather, can be enthralling.

To take this small gorge, in the middle of the most densely populated area of Canada, and call it a wilderness area may be stretching the term a little. But if by a wilderness one means a place where things that are living can go on living, with little or no disturbance from us, then the Spencer Gorge is by that definition a wilderness.

Take as one example the Eastern white cedar. It may, in fact, be the best example. Some of these trees grow on the rocky walls of the Escarpment, sustained by little more than the nutrients in the water washed down to them by the rain, yet they are the oldest living things east of the Rockies. The most elderly of them is a tree that was a seedling nearly 1,700 years ago, about the time the Romans stopped persecuting the Christians. (The remains of cedars dating back nearly 7,700 years have been found deep in the cold waters of Georgian Bay.) But these trees don't grow to be huge things, like the ancient trees of the Pacific coast, quite the opposite in fact. Scientists at the Cliff Ecology Research Group at the University of Guelph have studied 500-year-old specimens that are no bigger than a broomstick in diameter. Knowing even this little bit about the Eastern white cedar helps us appreciate that the Escarpment is more than a strip of wilderness—it's a sanctuary.

Borer's Falls

On Borer's Creek

Height – 16 m (52 ft)   Crest Width – 9 m (29 ft)   N 43:17:64 W 79:56:22

Borer's Falls Conservation Area
Royal Botanical Gardens

Best Time to View: Early spring and after periods of substantial rain. Borer's Creek doesn't provide this ribbon falls with a lot of water. It faces south and is open to the sky.

Responsible Authority:

Hamilton Region Conservation Authority, (905) 648-4427

Royal Botanical Gardens, (905) 825-5040

How to Get There: Follow Highway 403 from where it separates from the QEW and makes its way through the west end of Hamilton. Exit at Main Street and go west; it will change to Osler Drive and then back again to Main Street. Keep going. You'll soon come to King Street in Dundas. Turn left. As you drive through town, watch on your right for Sydenham Road (Hamilton-Wentworth Road 505). Turn right. This will eventually take you up the Escarpment. Keep going. Soon Sydenham Road will make a sharp turn to the right and then to the left. Don't make the turn to the left! Go straight. You'll find yourself on Rock Chapel Road. Borer's Falls is less than a kilometer away. There may or may not be a sign at the falls to indicate that you've found it. Look instead for a bridge with railings made of heavy wooden timbers. This spans the crest of the falls. There's room to park a couple of cars on the east side. The parking lot for the Rock Chapel Sanctuary is about 200 meters to the west. It's a better bet if you're planning to stay awhile.

If you stand on the bridge that crosses Borer's Creek and look beyond the crest of the falls, which is just feet away, you get a good view of the deep gorge that runs down into the conservation area and out to the woodlands of the Royal Botanical Gardens. If you cross the bridge and look in the opposite direction, you can see that the stream, as it exists today, is far too small to have made such a gorge. How was it able to summon such force? And how was the Borer family able to generate enough power from it to run a sawmill for 100 years, a mill that was the mainstay of the village of Rock Chapel? Questions! There are always more questions than answers when contemplating the mysteries of the Escarpment.

The creek bed north of the bridge is strangely different, too. At first glance it looks as if someone has lined it with cut stone. You wonder why. But then, as you study it more closely, you realize nature is the responsible party. Nevertheless, like

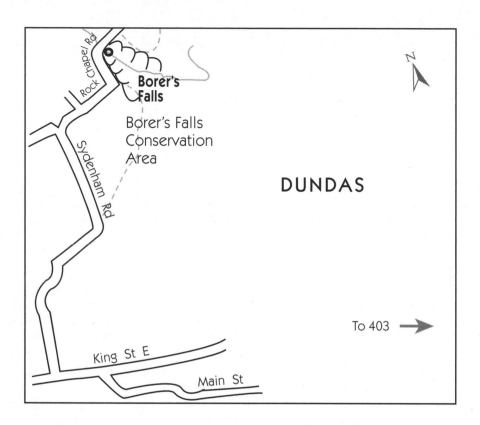

the Giant's Causeway in the north of Ireland, it looks too geometrically perfect to have been created by natural forces.

You can see more of this unusual stonework if you walk round the edge of the gorge to the east and go in among the trees. There you'll find gnarled old cedars growing out of stone walls, walls that look as if they were cut and set by a firm of master stonemasons. There are similar rocky outcroppings elsewhere along the Escarpment, but none imitate the handiwork of humans quite so admirably as here.

This is an easy waterfall to get close to. You can safely walk right onto the crest — after you fight your way through the snarl of lilacs that surrounds it! Most of the year you can ignore these shrubs as plain old scrubby *syringa vulgaris,* but for three weeks in May they make it a heavenly place to be. How ironic and sad that clumps of lilac that are often the only things left to mark the places where many pioneer families put down their roots in Canada.

And how paradoxical that the largest and finest collection of lilacs in the world should be just a couple of kilometers away from Borer's Falls, in the famous Lilac Dell at the Royal Botanical Gardens. The RBG operates the International Registry for all new varieties of the shrub, and during the spring lilac festival the sweet breath of spring is so heady you can almost taste it.

Webster's Falls is one of the most accessible and popular
on the Escarpment.

A February thaw leaves majestic Tews Falls in a sullen, misty mood.

Who would believe that Grindstone Falls was once a major industrial site?

Hilton Falls is a worthy destination at the end of a long trek
through the woods.

The ruins of one of Ontario's earliest hydroelectric plants at the Cataract.

Handsome Hogg's Falls in the Beaver Valley is one of the area's
least-known waterfalls.

Above: The village of Walter's Falls has a pair of
waterfalls as its centerpiece.
Below: Jones Falls is one of a trio of bright, showy waterfalls
at Owen Sound.

As evening shadows darken, Indian Falls takes on a look of rustic splendor.

Between the falls and the Lilac Dell the RBG has 1,092 hectares (2,700 acres) of gardens, woods, meadow and water. There are 50 kilometers of trails and a thousand species of plants, deer, fox, muskrat, coyotes, all safely protected in this oasis in the middle of the Golden Horseshoe. You can access it through the back door, so to speak, by taking the trail down the Escarpment from the Rock Chapel Sanctuary parking lot. On the way down you'll be treated to a spectacular view of distant Burlington Bay, the Skyway Bridge and the steel plants. In the foreground to the east you'll see the headlands of the Escarpment and the rolling countryside at its base. Say a little prayer as you take it all in, a prayer of thanks for the environmental activists in the 1920s who saved this area from becoming a quarry. Even in the most indifferent times there were always people who cared.

One of the best-known treasures of the RBG is the oddly named Cootes Paradise, the big pond that dominates the landscape of Hamilton's west end. Originally it was called Little Washquarter (Burlington Bay was Big Washquarter), but a certain British army officer spent so much time there hunting that people began to look upon it as his own preserve.

Elizabeth Posthuma Simcoe, wife of Lt. Gov. John Graves Simcoe, mentioned him in her diary when she and her husband visited Burlington Heights, June 6, 1796.

> Further west of this terrace we saw Coote's Paradise, so called from a Capt. Coote. Who spent a great deal of time in shooting ducks in this marshy tract of land below the hill we are upon. It abounds with wild fowl and tortoises; from hence it appears more like a river or a lake than a marsh, and Mordaunt's (Morden) Point in the distance takes a fine shape. I was so pleased with this place that the governor stayed and dined at Beasley's. A strong east wind prevented our sailing back. We therefore arrived late, and found a salmon and a tortoise ready dressed for our dinner.

Captain Coote was a member of the 8th King's Own Regiment. When he wasn't engaged in decimating the duck population he was busy superintending the building of Dundas Street through the tangled forests of Upper Canada. Coincidentally, when surveyors laid out the town of Dundas they called it Cootes Paradise. The name was changed after the road was built. It's too bad, in a way. The town could have enjoyed great celebrity alongside Moose Jaw and Medicine Hat on the list of Canadian communities with the zaniest names.

Grindstone Falls

On Grindstone Creek

Height – 6 m (20 ft)   Crest Width – 4.5 m (15 ft)   N 43:19:83 W 79:53:28

Best Time to View: Spring and winter. There's a viewing platform built right at
the brink. When the water's running high or there's lots of ice at the base and
around the edges of this little curtain falls, you'll feel right in the middle of
things. Grindstone faces south and is partly open to the sky.

Responsible Authority: Halton Region Conservation Authority, (905) 336-1158

How to Get There: Take the QEW to Exit 101 (Burlington). Go north on Brant
Street about 3.5 kilometers to what used to be Highway 5 but is now Halton
Road 5. (It will always be Dundas Street to some.) Turn left and go the short
distance into Waterdown. At Mill Street turn left again. Follow it downhill,
under a railway overpass, to a small park on the right. The falls is just steps
from the parking lot.

It's so easy to say Waterdown without thinking that it means *water down*. Of course
there's a waterfall here.

A legendary millwright from Albany, New York, Henry Van Wagner, gave the
name Waterdown to a flour mill he built here for the town's founder, Ebenezer
Culver Griffin. It came to him, apparently, after he spent an evening sitting, staring
at the falls. Perhaps it doesn't qualify as one of the great moment of eureka but it
was an enduring choice nevertheless.

Van Wagner built a number of mills along the Escarpment and must have
done well financially for he ended up owning the fine home of the colorful Augustus Jones. Van Wagner deserves to be remembered for other things. He once
performed the extraordinary and eccentric feat of rowing a boat across Canada.

The Waterdown Mill was the nucleus for a cluster of mills that were eventually
built around the falls. People called this little industrial complex Smokey Hollow,
and quite proudly so. Soot, grit and air pollution were badges of progress in the
19th century.

The mills at Smokey Hollow thrived for 100 years. They burn down from time
to time, some of them several times, but even in the days of no fire insurance and
timid bankers the owners usually found some way to rebuild.

A big fire in 1912 finally put the last of them out of business, though the decision of the railroad to bypass the town had already doomed it. Now when you
stand next to the falls and look around, there's barely a stone left to hint at what
once was there. The mills probably disappeared in the same way that many of the
great buildings of Rome disappeared: they became a convenient quarry. If you were

Waterdown's attractive Grindstone Falls.

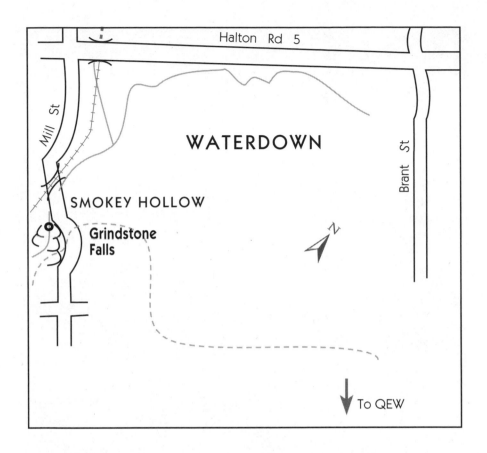

Map showing Halton Rd 5, Mill St, Brant St, WATERDOWN, SMOKEY HOLLOW, Grindstone Falls, and To QEW.

building something new, why would you cut fresh stones when you could find them ready-cut in the nearby ruins.

Grindstone Falls has been known at times as Great Falls. It is small, not nearly big enough to merit the name, though small in this case doesn't mean unattractive. Several descending layers of caprock at the crest make it quite a distinctive waterfall. You can see here, better than in other places, how the Wisconsin glacier abrasively scored the caprock. The rocks at the crest and the big blocks lying on the floor of the gorge have been deeply marked by the moving ice.

Below the falls, Grindstone Creek flows through a pleasant area of new-growth forest. Above it is a natural amphitheater. There's nothing but grass there now, but if the Halton Region Conservation Authority and the people of Waterdown ever decide to create an elegant civic park, they have the perfect site for it.

Grindstone is the last of the waterfalls concentrated around Hamilton. A short distance to the east is the distinctive promontory of Flamborough Head. There the Escarpment makes a sharp turn to the north. There are no more waterfalls of any great size until you get north of the 401.

Hilton Falls

On Sixteen Mile Creek

Height – 10 m (32.5 ft)   Crest Width – 6 m (19.5 ft)   N 43:30:53 W 79:58:83

Hilton Falls Conservation Area

Best Time to View: Because it flows through a fairly large area of maturing woods, Sixteen Mile Creek isn't as quick to dry up as other streams. That makes Hilton Falls a year-round attraction. Because of those woods, it is in deep shade much of the time. It's a curtain falls and faces south.

Responsible Authority: Halton Region Conservation Authority, (905) 336-1158

How to Get There: Take Highway 401 to Exit 312 (Campbellville). Go north on the Guelph Line (Halton Road 1). Almost immediately you'll come to the Campbellville Road (Halton Road 9). Turn right. It's a little more than 3 kilometers to Hilton Falls Conservation Area. There's lots of parking. Expect to pay a fee, even in winter when many people ski to the falls.

It was Thanksgiving Day, a day so close to perfection it would have been sacrilege not to have been openly thankful for every good thing you could think of — to be alive, to be in Canada, to be at Hilton Falls. Spirits were as balmy as the weather.

"Isn't this the most beautiful day?" people inquired of every group of passing strangers.

"Marvelous, just marvelous!" would come the reply.

As far ahead as we could see the trail was crowded with people. Hilton is farther from the road than any waterfall on the Escarpment — about 2 kilometers — and yet it's more popular at times than any of the others. That may be because it's the only waterfall of any size between Waterdown and the Forks of the Credit, a 60-kilometer stretch. And it may be because the Halton Region Conservation Authority goes out of its way to make a visit to the falls a pleasant experience.

The path is wide and well groomed, and on most days they keep a fire burning in the pit next to the falls. That appeals to people, even in summer when the smell of wood smoke is the only good reason for having one. The display boards at the falls are among the best written and best illustrated at any attraction. And a graceful set of stairs runs down the side of the gorge to give people access to the base of the falls, perhaps more to keep them from being tempted to take the dangerous way down than for their convenience.

Maybe because it was a holiday, maybe because the weather was such an irresistible lure, but we saw a lot of people on the trail that day we wouldn't ordinarily expect to find in the woods. Some were wearing shoes that were little better than slippers. Others looked far from fit enough to be there. The mix was worthy of

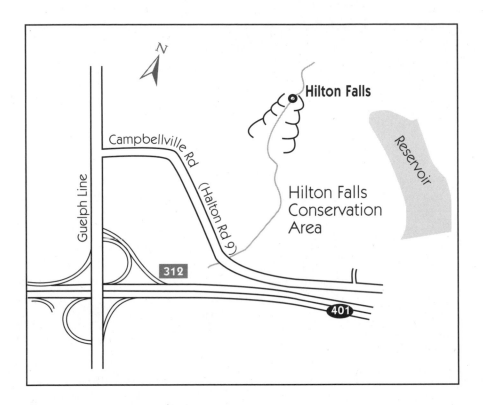

Yonge Street — Caucasian, African, Latin and Asian in all the many varieties. We heard Chinese, Spanish and a surprising amount of Russian as we passed. One large group of people, possibly from the same family, passed us on bicycles, the adults speaking French, the children speaking English. We couldn't hear those who hurried by on horseback. Some looked unmistakably Anglo-Saxon, others distinctively Teutonic.

Not everyone made it to the falls. The numbers thinned noticeably after we had gone a kilometer or so. We figured it wasn't because the dropouts were unable to go further but because it had finally dawned on them that every kilometer forward was a kilometer they had to walk back.

Still, Hilton Falls was a busy place when we got there. The water level was still a little low from the summer drought and people were walking about on the crest of the falls, something they wouldn't ordinarily be able to do. At the base of the falls, children were having great fun walking in behind the falling water.

Others were clamoring about the stonework that once supported an enormous waterwheel. It was unusual in that it was a flutter or undershot wheel rather than the more common overshot. It apparently was a beautifully crafted thing of iron and wood that by some accounts may have been as large as 40 feet in diameter, though others suggest the actual dimension was somewhere around 25 feet. It weighed 3,500 pounds.

Foundation of the old mill at Hilton Falls.

Hilton Falls.

We got down at the level of the stream bed and studied the stonework, trying to imagine how the sawmill would have looked as it hugged the wall of the gorge next the falls. It must have been a beautiful thing. Even today the stone arch through which the water was expelled back into the stream is a thing to be admired. There isn't a lick of mortar in it and yet it has stood there for 165 years without shifting or moving, held in place by nothing but the magic of gravity.

We climbed up onto the rocks above the ruins and look down into the well that had held the waterwheel. There, if one had any doubts, was incontrovertible proof that the mill had been out of operation since the year Canada became a nation. There was a huge cedar growing horizontally out of the side of the gorge, just about where the hub of the wheel would have been.

The sawmill was built in 1835 by Edward Hilton, who soon became involved in the Rebellion of 1837 — on the losing side! He fled Canada, into exile and oblivion. The waterfall has preserved his name for posterity but that appears to be all he got out of the enterprise. The mill fell into other hands. In 1867 it burned and was never replaced. The great wheel was sold for scrap, for $30, to pay back taxes.

The whole time we were there Mikal never once reached for his camera, though I knew he was tempted. He wanted the waterfall in solitude, not when it was overrun with people. He returned the next day on his own, a day that was only a little less lovely than the one before, and had the falls pretty well to himself. The only people out and about were those you'd expect to find in the woods at that time of year — the intrepid seniors.

The Cataract

On the Credit River

Height – 14 m (45.5 ft)   Crest Width – 9 m (29ft)   N 43:49:24 W 80:01:29

Forks of the Credit Provincial Park

Best Time to View: Only an exceptional summer dry spell will deprive you of the best this curtain falls has to offer. The Credit River isn't a big stream, especially this far north, but thanks to the many wooded areas in its watershed it does run well. The falls faces southwest and is open to the sky.

Responsible Authority:

Ministry of Natural Resources, Ontario Parks, 1-800-667-1940

How to Get There: Go north on Highway 10 to the Charleston Sideroad (Peel Road 24). Turn left. In a few minutes you'll come to Cataract Road (Peel Road 3). Turn left again. In a minute or so you'll reach the Cataract Inn. Turn right. The entrance to the provincial park and the path to the falls are about 100 meters further along on your left. Don't park your car in front of the gate! There's enough loose gravel there to bury you right to the axles. The only place you'll be going is back up the road to the English call box in front of the inn to phone for a tow truck to come and winch you out. (Does it sound like we speak from experience?) Elsewhere the village is a forest of No Parking signs. The message is clear.

You can, of course, make a left off the Charleston Sideroad onto McLaren Road and go south to the main gate where there is a parking lot. All you'll have to do then is trek 5 kilometers or so to the falls and back. It's a delightful hike, if it's a hike you want. If it isn't, consider having lunch or dinner at the Cataract Inn, (519) 927-3033, then you can confidently leave your car in their lot and visit the falls before or after you've eaten.

For 200 years the Credit River was a major north-south highway for traders and explorers. From its source near Orangeville it flows more or less directly south, running parallel to Highway 10 all the way to Mississauga, where it empties into Lake Ontario. The name comes not from someone offering goods in advance of payment but a French fur trader from Lachine whose name was Credit. The river's watershed was his territory.

The Cataract is more deeply undermined than any other waterfall on the Escarpment. There's a real cave behind it. Some day water and frost will have their way with the big slab of dolostone that bridges the crest and it will crack and collapse. That will alter the character of the falls dramatically, perhaps even transform it from a curtain falls into a cascade.

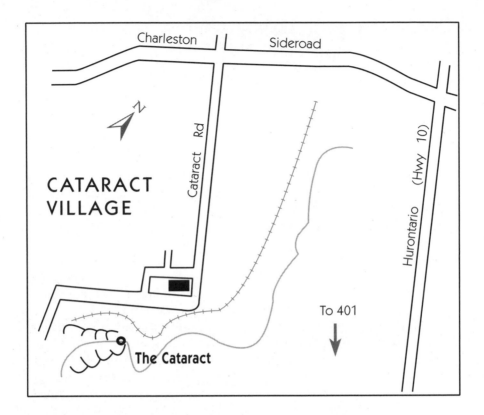

The village of Cataract has already been transformed from its former bustling self to its present sleepy self. Aside from the pretty country inn there isn't much else to it. Long gone are the dreams of a succession of men who wanted to turn it into a metropolis.

The first was a young man from Toronto named William Grant who came looking for gold in 1818. Geology was an infant science then and a lot of people thought that any exposed area of rock was a likely place to find the precious metal. Grant didn't find gold but when he stooped to take a drink from a pool of water he discovered something almost as valuable — salt! Nowadays, thanks to huge deposits beneath the cities of Windsor and Sarnia, we can afford to treat salt with a nonchalance that borders on carelessness. In the 19th century, however, and for centuries before that, salt, which was used extensively for preserving meat and vegetables, was an expensive commodity.

Grant persuaded a former employer to put up money to develop a mine near the falls. As it turned out, there wasn't enough salt to warrant the effort, but he did build a sawmill and several other buildings, enough to give the place a name and a rather pretty name at that — Gleniffer.

Gleniffer didn't exist for very long. It was soon abandoned and left to molder away until 1858 when Richard Church bought the entire community for $100 and changed the name to Church's Falls. In a couple of years he had a sawmill, a gristmill and a woolen mill going and was manufacturing barrels and brooms and beer. He laid out 160 building lots and named the streets of the prospective town after his children.

The Credit River Railroad arrived in the late 1870s to make the place even more prosperous. The rail line still runs along the west side of the falls. About the only sour note for Mr. Church was the rail company's insistence that he change the name of the town to Cataract. They thought Church's Falls would be confused with Churchville, which was at the other end of the line.

For years there were four passenger trains a day to Cataract. In the 1880s, freight traffic was especially heavy, as large shipments of the area's distinctive red stone were sent to Toronto to build the Ontario Legislature and various colleges at the University of Toronto.

The mill nearest the falls burned — a couple of times. In 1885, John Deagle, who was an inventor, among other things, bought the scorched shell for $1,800

The ruins of the power plant at the Cataract give it an air of mystery.

and rebuilt it as hydroelectric generating station, one of the earliest in Canada. He was the first person in the country to construct a generator that featured a revolving field, the kind still in use today.

Deagle began operation in 1892 and was soon supplying power to local farms. Grateful farmers, who had never known anything but muscle power and the light of kerosene lamps, must have thought it a miracle. Later he began construction of a tunnel that he hoped would increase the head — the height of the water drop — from 14 meters to 51 meters. It was destroyed in the spring floods of 1912, a fate that befell similar projects along the Escarpment.

The hydro plant changed hands several times but continued to be the power source for Hillsburgh, Caledon, Caledon East, Inglewood, the Cheltenham Brickworks and Orangeville until 1947. In 1953, Ontario Hydro dynamited the building. Today the ruins give a ghostly atmosphere to the falls.

The remains of the power plant are surrounded by a rusty chain-link fence. It keeps people out of what is obviously a dangerous and unstable place but one wishes that something more aesthetically appropriate had been used. Americans complain that too many of their waterfalls have been fenced off in this manner. Ontarians are more fortunate. With the exception of Chedoke and the Cataract, the waterfalls of the Escarpment have largely escaped this kind of abuse.

We would be happier too if the bridge leading to the falls and the viewing platform were not made of a heavy-duty welded steel that is more suitable for highway construction than providing access to something as benign and graceful as a waterfall. To make things worse, you can't see much of the falls from the viewing platform. That serves only to frustrate visitors and send them round to the other side, onto the railroad tracks, to get a better view.

There's no pleasure in knocking the Ministry of Natural Resources. It is, after all, responsible for some of Ontario's most cherished treasures — our provincial parks. Nevertheless, it's a shame a more delicate hand couldn't have been put to work at the Cataract.

Hogg's Falls

On the Boyne River

Height – 6 m (19.5 ft)   Crest Width – 10 m (32.5 ft)   N 44:16:23   W 80:32:31

Hogg's Falls Resource Management Area

Best Time to View: The Boyne is not a major river but it does run through a good stretch of cedar forest before it tumbles over the Escarpment. That's assurance water levels will usually be pretty good. It's a classic curtain falls facing north and is shaded somewhat.

Responsible Authority:

Ministry of Natural Resources, Ontario Parks, 1-800-667-1940

How to Get There: Go north of Shelburne on Highway 10 to Flesherton. At the crossroads in the village, turn right onto Grey County Road 4. In two or three minutes you'll come to East Back Line. Turn left. A short drive through a thick cedar forest will bring you to a spot where the road forks. Go right, onto Lower Valley Road. Soon you'll come to a long, lazy curve and then a number of cart tracks leading into the woods on the left. Two of these have yellow gates. Either one will take you to the falls. It's only a minute's walk. There's room to park just one car in front of each gate

William Hogg, whose kin were pioneer millers in several communities in Southern Ontario, including the familiar Hogg's Hollow in Toronto, gave his name to this falls, though he's remembered most for the grand schemes he attempted down the road at Eugenia Falls.

If you get a little downstream from the falls and look at it from a certain angle, you'll recognize it instantly as the classic waterfall of the tourist brochure. Only the fly fisherman in hipwaders, drawing a taut line across dark, swirling waters, is missing from this otherwise perfect scene.

Here the swift-flowing Boyne River is broad but shallow. To the innocent eye it certainly looks like the kind of stream fish might inhabit. Whether or not there are fish in the pool below the falls is a question that can't be reliably answered by two men who've never seen a trout up close that didn't have a sprig of parsley parked next to it.

It truly is a lovely waterfall. A gossamer fount of sparkling water that falls ever so gently into the clearest of pools. Except for a single large boulder, which may well have been chipped away by frost, there's no talus or rock debris about the base. That's part of why it looks so clean and attractive.

The surrounding gorge is a perfect setting. Along Lower Valley Road and upstream the forest is thick with cedar, but here in the vicinity of the falls the woods are a mix of deciduous and coniferous, open and nicely sloped to the water's edge.

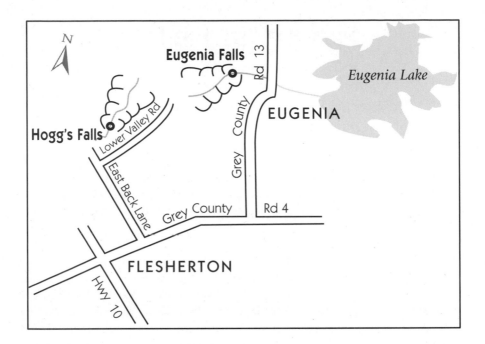

The lane leading in from the yellow gates is a leftover from yesteryear. Until well after the Second World War many roads in rural Ontario looked a lot like this one. It doesn't take much imaginative effort to conjure up visions of a couple of draft horses tugging a load of heavy timbers to the mill, or a prancing little mare pulling a sleigh or a cutter, or a Model A or Model T put-putting along through the trees.

Among the waterfalls of the Escarpment this one is an exception in that its face appears to be made up entirely of caprock — the hard Lockport dolostone that forms only the top layer at other falls. There's no undermining and no evidence of the soft shale that usually constitutes the second layer. Here, at the extreme southern end of the Beaver Valley, the caprock appears to be thicker than at other places, thicker than anywhere except at Niagara Falls, where it is an astonishing 25 meters thick.

Upstream there's a relatively small dam made of poured concrete. It's clear from this that the mill at Hogg's Falls never was a very big enterprise. The center of the dam is open now and the water runs freely through it. In the past, when they wanted to build up the water level in the millpond, they dropped heavy planks into this opening. The force of the river's flow held them in place.

The day they built the dam must have been a long one. Back then there were no ready-mix trucks to call. When they were finished, as dusk was gathering, someone thoughtfully scratched "Sept. 23, 1935" in the wet concrete. We can be certain it was dusk because soon after a raccoon, who wouldn't have been up and about until it was almost dark, left his own mark for posterity by walking through the wet concrete along the top of the dam.

Eugenia Falls

On the Beaver River

Height – 22 m (71.5 ft)   Crest Width – 12 m (39 ft)   N 44:18:89   W 80:31:70

Eugenia Falls Conservation Area

Best Time to View: Eugenia is but a trickle of its former self, with most of its water source long ago diverted for power generation. It wouldn't be worth visiting if it weren't for its spectacular setting and lovely surroundings. It's a ribbon falls facing south, open to the sky.

Responsible Authority: Grey Sauble Conservation Authority, (519) 376-3076

How to Get There: Go north of Shelburne on Highway 10 to Flesherton. At the crossroads in the village turn right, onto Grey County Road 4. Go east for five minutes or so till you come to Grey County Road 13. You'll see a sign on your right indicating the way to Eugenia and the conservation area. Turn left. The village is about 4 kilometers. Once there turn left on Pellisier Street. This will take you down to the parking lot.

The first European to see Eugenia Falls was a man named Brownlee. He was out hunting deer one day in 1852 and had drifted several miles through the wilderness to the west of the fledgling settlement of Artemesia, now the village of Flesherton, when he heard the sound of falling water. He must have been excited as he worked his way to the brink of the falls to observe his discovery. In the coming days and weeks he would get a lot more excited.

He returned a couple of days later to show a neighbor his spectacular find. They approached the falls from below. As they were climbing over the big blocks of broken caprock that marred their way, they suddenly spotted what looked like flecks of gold embedded in the stone. They had struck it rich.

The two tried to be secretive about it, perhaps too secretive. Others soon became suspicious of them and quickly the word gold was on everybody's lips. Within days the roar of the falls was punctuated by the ringing of hammers as dozens of men labored to extract the precious metal. In three weeks there were 200 of them hacking furiously at the rocks. It was then, however, that a more practiced eye, having looked closely at the ore, declared the bright flecks to be iron pyrite — fool's gold!

The broad, deep gorge below the falls, with its soaring rock walls, resembles what Americans of the Southwest would call a box canyon. The phrase describes it well, though it has long been known as the Cuckoo Valley. The name is not a comment on the mental state of Brownlee and his fellow gold-seekers but recognition of the fact that the black-billed cuckoo finds it a favorite nesting ground when it returns from wintering in Florida.

It was surveyors who gave the falls its name. They surely had to be among the most interesting men in the colony and, with few exceptions, the most traveled. Many had served in the armies of the world — that's where they no doubt had learned the trade — and had been to the farthest of faraway places, places like Samoa and Tierra del Fuego. They knew their Carlyle and their Tennyson and the classics and they often bestowed worldly names on the bucolic features they discovered in the Canadian wilderness.

It was a Frenchman who had served in the Crimean with the forces of Louis Napoleon who suggested the name. The others in the survey party wanted to call it Gibraltar Falls but he had a soft spot for Empress Eugenie de Montijo, Louis Napoleon's consort. Royalty in the 19th century were as popular as movie stars in the 20th century, and Eugenie, who set the fashion trends of the day, was as popular as any. She was, in fact, a bullheaded, imperious first lady who stood in the way of every move toward freedom or democracy. When she and Louis were deposed, they fled to England, to the village of Chiselhurst. She lived for another 50 years, dying in 1920. One wonders if she was ever told that someone had named a beautiful waterfall in Canada after her — and that they had got her name wrong! Who knows whether that had something to do with the Frenchman's accent or was just a case of poor handwriting. Eugenia Falls it is and always has been.

This was one of the last areas in the colony to be settled. It's the highest point of land in Southern Ontario. Several rivers, including the Saugeen, the Beaver, the Nottawasaga and the Grand, begin as brooks and springs in adjacent Osprey Township. None of these streams was full enough to carry people and goods to market. The surrounding forest, on the other hand, was almost impenetrable. How was a farmer to sell his harvest? How, indeed, was a settler to get his household goods to the land allotted to him?

Eventually, people came and settled anyway, determined people. Intrepid is not too strong a word for them. Consider a Mrs. Hewitt of Eugenia, who once walked the 140 kilometers to Toronto on her own, trudging through a forest that must have been forever intimidating and at times frightening, especially in the night. When she got to town she bought her husband a new pair of boots, filled them with essentials for her kitchen, strapped them to her back, and trudged back home again.

It took well over 100 years to rid Southern Ontario of its forests. Men and women seemed to be at it their whole lives. Two or three professional woodchoppers, working with nothing but axes, could clear an acre in as little as 10 days. That was as fast as anyone could go. It meant bringing down and disposing of huge first-growth trees. In nearby Flesherton there were 50 teams of horses at work hauling timber. In the year Brownlee discovered the waterfall, one of his neighbors wrote home to the old country to inform everyone that he had removed the trunk of an oak that was 144 feet long and had sold a 60-foot length of elm for $1.50. (There's a large, well-preserved stump of white pine in the museum at Owen Sound. A count of the rings when the tree was cut down revealed that it was a seedling in 1712.)

The village of Eugenia was founded in 1858 by the Purdy brothers. They built a house at the brink of the falls and by 1860 there were four mills operating there. The Purdys kept a general store that was filled with curios, including a pile of fool's gold nuggets to intrigue visitors. They also had the antlers from an enormous bull moose who had tumbled over the falls. They told stories of other animals who had gone to their deaths the same way, including a tale about a dog who had chased a deer over the brink. Both perished.

William Hogg, who gave his name to Hogg's Falls, came to Eugenia in 1870 to run a sawmill. Like John Deagle at the Cataract, he was quick to grasp the new science of electricity. In 1895 he bought a turbine and built a hydroelectric generating plant at the falls. It could produce 70 kilowatts, enough power to supply Eugenia and Flesherton plus several mills and nearby farms. Many farmers in the province didn't get electricity until 50 or 60 years later.

Hogg didn't stop there. He offered to upgrade the plant and transmit power to Toronto to run the city's streetcars. Others were proposing to do the same — using power generated at Niagara. The two water sources were about equidistant but the folks in Toronto may have had difficulty believing the modest waters of Eugenia could do the job. They chose Niagara.

In 1907 the Georgian Bay Power Company revived William Hogg's dream. They cut a large, very expensive tunnel through the big hill on the west side of the falls. The plan was to divert water from the falls to a generating plant on the other side of it. The tunnel cost a million dollars and was the work of the Franceschini Brothers, one of the first of the many Italian construction companies to leave their mark on a growing Canada. The arched entrance to the tunnel is still standing. The fine stonework looks as if it could last 1,000 years. As for the tunnel itself, a fierce flood destroyed it soon after and Georgian Bay Power went into bankruptcy.

In 1914, Ontario Hydro took over, building a dam above the falls and creating Eugenia Lake to feed yet another generating plant. That plant is still operating and boasts the highest head, or water drop, of any power plant east of the Rockies — 125 meters — but it uses up most of the water once destined for the waterfall. The world has passed Eugenia by. Its industries are gone. Now the village is just a scattering of houses.

Seeing Mikal intent as usual on finding some elusive new angle from which to photograph the falls, I got out of his way. I followed the sunshine down an inviting path that runs along the edge of the gorge. On one side was a high, handsome stone wall that enabled me to lean safely forward to look deep into the valley below. On the other side were some of the most oddly gnarled and twisted old cedars I had ever seen.

The trees were the ubiquitous Eastern white cedar, of course. Many people still call them arbor vitae. In 1535, when Jacques Cartier landed at the spot where Quebec City now stands, his men were suffering terribly from scurvy. Twenty-five had

All that's left of a million-dollar dream at Eugenia Falls.

already died and others were near death. The Indians urged them to drink a tea they had brewed from cedar. Miraculously, Cartier's crew recovered almost instantly and hence the name arbor vitae — the tree of life. The Eastern white cedar, it would seem, is loaded with Vitamin C.

After a while I turned away from the gorge and followed a side path through the woods. I could hear the faint sound of the wind in the trees overhead, the sound one always hears in a cedar grove, winter or summer. You hear it even when the wind doesn't appear to be blowing at all.

All around me was evidence of the silent struggle that goes on between trees and rocks, a struggle that must have lasted for eons. Surprisingly, the trees were frequently the winners, wrestling life, sometimes a long life, from the very stones themselves. One fine old specimen, for example, had split a large boulder neatly in two with its growth. There didn't appear to be a speck of soil to give it sustenance.

There was little soil to be seen anywhere. It takes a long time, sometimes as much as 1,000 years, to make an inch of topsoil. Yet trees had long sprouted and prospered here. They truly are the great survivors of the plant kingdom, only mosses, lichens and ferns have been around longer. As for the rocks, they looked like they'd been through their own agonies. Mikal took to calling them popcorn rocks because of their puffy, twisted shapes.

On the other side of the cedar grove I came upon a modest little memorial to the men of Eugenia who had served in the wars. It was the last thing I expected to

A sunny path at Eugenia Falls.

find there, though there couldn't have be a more appropriately peaceful place to honor and remember them.

I stood there for a minute or two, staring up at the figure atop the monument. A robin chirped comfortingly in the big maple overhead. The statue was a life-sized replica of a young soldier. It seemed almost human, the epitome of earnestness and innocence. He was just a boy. They had all been just boys.

As I read the names inscribed in the stone below, I felt a rush of sadness. On the south side, the sunny side, was a list of those who came home to Eugenia when the Great War was over. On the north side, forever in shadow, were those who had died. In the sunlight I could read the names of the Hoys, the Fishers, the three Osbornes. Josiah Parliament was there, too, but those of Earl and Stanley Parliament were on the other side, the dark side. Were they his brothers? Imagine going off to war with your brothers and coming home alone!

On the side of the monument, on a small, crowded tablet that looked like it had been added as an afterthought, were the names of those who had fought in the Second World War. When they planned the memorial they hadn't provided room for subsequent wars. In 1918 they truly believed they had fought the war to end all wars.

As I walked back through the cedar grove, drawn by the peaceful, soothing sound of the waterfall, I thought about another alluring sound, the pied piper sound of patriotism that had enticed all those young men to leave this lovely, shining place. Even when it's uttered in innocence, patriotism can be the cruelest trickery.

Lavender Falls

We tried to find this waterfall on one occasion, without success. We mistakenly went looking for it around the hamlet of Lavender. That's not where it is.

We put off the search till another day when there would be more time, then put it off permanently after receiving a letter from Peter Thompson, secretary of the Blue Mountains Club of the Bruce Trail Association. He informed us that the falls "used to be accessible from the Bruce Trail but is now strictly closed to the public due to erosion of the banks by too many careless visitors." We learned later they had even built stairs at the falls to alleviate the problem, to no avail.

The environment is far more fragile around some waterfalls than others. Members of the Bruce Trail Club locate the trail where they believe it will do the least harm. If subsequent use threatens the environment, they move it. It's best to trust their good judgment and follow the trail as marked.

There's one other waterfall we haven't included, one we did find. It's one of the most unusual and one of the most beautiful. We knew it was on private property when we went looking for it but we also knew we could access it from an unopened public road allowance that runs along the front of it. It was breathtaking — two upper falls and a lower one separated by long stretches of rapids in an unblemished wilderness setting.

We began to question the wisdom of including it after we learned something of its history. At one time it was accessible to the public and some people badly mistreated it. Cars tore up the ground around the falls and people dumped garbage into the gorge. The current owners stopped that when they bought the property and began the long task of cleaning up. It took years but slowly they brought it back to perfection. Now it's a veritable sanctuary for creatures such as the vulnerable Louisiana waterthrush, which is rarely found in Southwestern Ontario.

Places and things to be preserved usually fare best in public hands, but there are some circumstances in which the private owner appears to be the better custodian. This is one of them. So, with great reluctance, we made the decision not to reveal the location of this exceptional waterfall. It didn't seem like the fair thing to do.

A magnificent waterfall on a private property.

Anthea's Falls

On Minniehill Creek

Height – 2 m (6.5 ft)   Crest Width – 3 m (9.5 ft)   N 44:30:36   W 80:37:20

Rocklyn Creek Management Area

Best Time to View: Spring and fall. Minniehill Creek is just a rivulet but then Anthea's is a tiny waterfall; it doesn't need a lot of water to put on a good show. It's a cascade facing north and it's shaded.

Responsible Authority: Grey Sauble Conservation Authority, (519) 376-3976

How to Get There: Take Highway 10 to Markdale, which is about halfway between Shelburne and Owen Sound. Turn right onto Grey County Road 12. Go north approximately 25 kilometers to Grey County Road 4 and the hamlet of Blantyre. There's room to park several cars on the grass at the community center.

Anthea's Falls is about 1.5 kilometers east on the Bruce Trail. If the weather's right, it's a hike you'll enjoy. This stretch is typical of many on the trail, with a mix of woods and farmland and little evidence of the Escarpment until you reach the falls. It's here, when you're away from the grandeur of cliffs and headlands, that you really come to appreciate what a prodigious achievement the Bruce Trail is. From start to finish it's longer than the distance from Windsor to Ottawa, and every step of it has had to be negotiated and secured by agreements with the owners of private property and the administrators of over 100 parks and conservation areas. The Bruce Trail Association has over 8,000 members who quite rightly take a proprietary interest in its well-being, ensuring that it is always carefully marked and free of litter and, most of all, never loses its naturalness to overdevelopment.

The community center at Blantyre is an aging but virtuous-looking building that served for many years as the meeting place for the local Women's Institute. There's a rusty mailbox at the bottom of the lane. On it we could just make out the words Allinson's Falls. It was some weeks before we learned how and why it became Anthea's Falls.

At the back of the property, where we picked up the Bruce Trail going east, someone had thoughtfully placed a sign telling hikers there was a spring behind the community center, if they wanted to clean up or refresh themselves before trekking on.

The way to the falls is mostly through new-growth forest, though there is one quite open section along the back of a cornfield that is shaded by magnificent old maple and beech trees. If you love trees, there has to be a special place in your heart for beech. They seem as aged and unchanging as the rocks themselves. Grey County

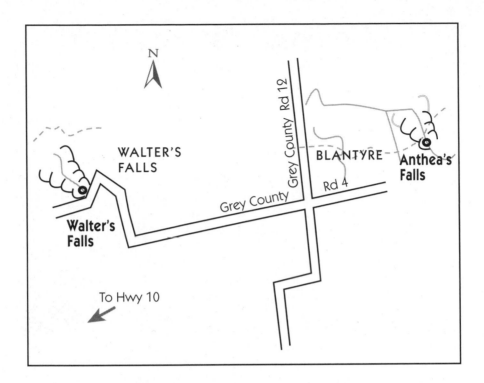

has more than its share of beech, including a good many that are first growth.

I wondered, as we admired one stand of beech in particular, what it is that compels people to use this species as a notice board for inscribing public pronouncements of love. One such proclamation was dated 1947, though the tree itself had to be at least 100 years older than that.

Along the edge of the field and around the base of the trees was the most imposing collection of boulders I think I've ever seen. They made me appreciate, if I hadn't before, what a Herculean task it was to clear the land not just of trees but of stones. If one could tally the sweat and curses that went into this great pile. Some of the boulders were simply too big to have been wrestled onto stone boats and dragged here by oxen or horses. Only a tractor, and a powerful one at that, could have moved them. Twice we crossed fences on stiles. Nothing still in use today seems quite so old fashioned or so simple and practical.

We came upon the little falls almost before we knew it, the sound of gently falling water capturing our attention just as we were about to step down into the shallow hollow. The prettiest part was upstream, in the shadows of the forest, where the water dances down a long series of limestone steps that runs on for at least 50 meters.

As to why the name of the falls was changed from Allinson's to Anthea's, the mystery was solved for us by a letter we received from Tom East of Waterloo, Ontario.

Tiny Anthea's Falls is a memorial to a lost daughter.

Tom is typical of the people who conceived the Bruce Trail and who, starting in 1967, put it all together, piece by piece. I should say more than typical, because he became president of the association in 1969 and started the Escarpment Preservation Fund, the means by which a good deal of land along the trail has since been put securely into public hands. He took a deep personal interest in the property that contains the little waterfall and even put up some of his own money to purchase it. On the day they dedicated it, he and members of the Beaver Valley Club rolled a huge boulder to the edge of the falls and stood it on end. Tom affixed a small bronze plaque to the top of it, a plaque that says:

> In memory of the beautiful, gentle Anthea
> Anthea Catherine East 'Ace', 1948–71

Anthea was Tom East's daughter, a daughter who had hiked the trail often with her parents and her sister, Vivian. In 1971, when she was only 23, she was killed while cycling in the south of France. For 14 years, Tom and his second wife, Isabel, maintained the 4 kilometers of the trail east of Blantyre in her memory.

Standing next to the little waterfall, looking at the forest growing up around it, seeing how the sun peers shyly through the trees to illuminate the water where it skips daintily over the stones, you know there couldn't have been a more endearing or enduring tribute to Anthea.

Walter's Falls

On Walter's Creek

Height – 12 m (40 ft)   Crest Width – 15 m (49 ft)   N 44:29:22   W 80:42:51

Best Time to View: All year round. A dam maintains water levels for the grist-mill, which is just upstream. The outflow feeds these side-by-side curtain falls. They face north and are open to the sky.

How to Get There: Go north of Flesherton on Highway 10 to Grey County Road 4, which is just south of Chatsworth. Turn right. Follow this road for 17 kilometers to the village of Walters Falls. At the intersection of Front and Victoria Streets you'll find the little community's only store. The gristmill is in the hollow at the bottom of Victoria. Turn right onto Front and follow it till you come to a large concrete slab. This is where the sawmill stood before it burned down in 1984. The falls are just steps away. You'll be able to hear them.

It was Saturday afternoon and there wasn't a soul on the streets of Walter's Falls. Somewhere in or around this quietest of quiet villages there had to be a waterfall. Why else the name? We drove around, hoping to discover it by happenstance. That's not always the surest way to one's objective but it does give you a quick sense of the character of a strange town.

Our first try brought us to St. Philip's Anglican Church, a tiny house of worship of commanding beauty. The words of Rupert Brooke came to mind as I admired it: "That there's some corner of a foreign field that is for ever England.… " I'm taking his words out of context by quoting them, I know. He was writing about fellow countrymen, fallen in battle and buried far from English shores. Still, the little church looked so English the poet's words just seemed to attach themselves to it.

Over the wall, in the churchyard, we could see the name "Walter" on the tallest of the tombstones. It was plain to us, however, in this corner of town, which is a little uphill, there is no waterfall.

We doubled back and made a turn at the crossroads. Down in the hollow, a couple of blocks away, there was a mill. That had to be it.

As we pulled up we could see it was as deserted as everything else in Walter's Falls. It was Saturday afternoon, after all, the time when old-fashioned businesses in the country traditionally close their doors for the weekend.

The mill site would have been as silent as the churchyard if it hadn't been for the multitude of sparrows chattering away in the eaves. What a favored lot they were. The moment they felt hungry all they had to do was open their wings and parachute to the ground, where there were enough oats scattered in the dust to feed ten times their number. It's a wonder any of them even bothered to learn how to fly.

On the bulletin board, next to the loading dock, there was a notice that some-body had a litter of potbelly pigs for sale and a reminder that Amber Waves was still in the business of custom combining.

Behind the mill there was a substantial dam and a large millpond. We learned later that this is one of the few working mills still powered by water. It is not a museum piece. Between the dam and the mill, the water in the creek tumbled tamely over two or three layers of caprock. It was academic whether we were look-ing at a waterfall or a rapid. Perhaps the original Walter's Falls was buried under the dam or beneath the waters of the millpond. Mikal took pictures of this "falls" anyway, though neither of us could muster much enthusiasm for it.

There's only one store in Walter's Falls, appropriately called The Store. We climbed the steps to a wooden porch and let ourselves in through the screen door. Inside, a man about my age, with a round, pleasant face and a thatch of gray hair, was reminiscing with the woman behind the counter. He nodded and politely stopped talking while she poured us coffee. Then we, too, were drawn into the con-versation as he continued. He told us about how after the war, in England, he sat down one day and ate his very first coconut and read *Moby Dick* for the first time.

"I enjoyed it so much that ever since, every ten years or so, I get myself a coconut and I take down my copy of *Moby Dick* and I do it all over again."

It was a charming story. And he was a charming man. He introduced himself as Wally and we traded tales. As we talked I couldn't help but be distracted by a picture on the wall next to him, a framed photograph of a most beautiful waterfall — twin waterfalls, in fact, flowing side-by-side.

I tried to put the question as delicately as I could, not wanting to admit we had come to a village as small as this one and not been able to find Walter's Falls. "That waterfall on the wall? How far is it if we wanted to go and have a look at it?"

"I'll take you there myself," Wally announced. "Follow me!" He slapped an old canvas hat on the back of his head and was out the door even before I could fish enough money out of my pocket to pay for the coffee. As we were leaving, the woman behind the counter smiled and handed us a bumper sticker, compliments of the house. We smiled, too. It said: I Was Lost in Walter's Falls.

Wally circled in front of us with his 4 X 4 and then off he scooted. It wasn't far. We could have walked the distance in five minutes. But we were grateful to him, nevertheless, for his guidance and his company — and for showing us places in the gorge that we might never had found on our own.

There's a wooden viewing platform built right over the crest of Walter's Falls. Walking on it is a bit of an adventure, however. Some of the floorboards have rot-ted pretty badly. From it you can look directly down on these two dazzling waterfalls.

Wally told us that the Walter in the name came from John Walter. The story, as he heard it — though he was quick to caution it was hearsay — was that in 1850 young John was a gardener on a big estate in England. He and one of the girls from the family that lived in the big house fell in love. The only way for the two of them to secure a happy ending in such circumstances was to run away together. And so they ran — thousands of miles away — to what must have been an enchanting bit of virgin wilderness, a place where no one could force them apart. Here they could make a good life for themselves and prosper. They could also play a seminal role in creating a new world for the generations to come, though their dreams may not have been grand enough to encompass something as noble as that.

Already I could visualize the final scene of the movie, with the two of them standing together on the spot where we now stood, their eyes fixed proudly and possessively on the waterfalls. Wally took that image away from me in a hurry. John and the missus didn't even know these waterfalls existed, not in the beginning, at least, for they settled at a much smaller waterfall nearby. It was sometime later, when John was out one day looking for a lost cow, that he came upon this spectacular site. He would have been a fool not to have moved everything here and started over again. And John Walter apparently was no fool, even if he had taken longer to find Walter's Falls than we did.

Mikal wanted to get pictures from below the falls, and Wally led us past several old abandoned-looking buildings and around some rusty industrial pieces that must have come from the sawmill. Then we were on a lovely lane that must have been a logging road at one time, descending through a cedar forest to the bottom of the gorge. As we walked Wally told us he had been a schoolteacher but had long since retired to the country. I asked if he was a farmer then. He smiled and said no, he just lived on a farm.

Near the bottom we left the lane and finished our descent on a path that was almost too fantastic to be believed. We passed between two huge blocks of stone, each as big as a house. They were composed of layers of rock so finely fitted together you'd swear they were the work of humans. They were perfectly parallel to each other and the way between them couldn't have been cut more perfectly if nature had worked from a blueprint.

We were surrounded on all sides by rock and moss and fern. There was such a seductive air of mystery about the place that anyone with a well-tuned fancy might be persuaded to go looking for the little people, who surely could be found foxing about somewhere in the undergrowth. At this point Wally bid us a cheerful good-bye. I couldn't help thinking that he looked like a bit of a leprechaun himself as he climbed back up the path.

The two waterfalls were even more imposing from below, especially with the sun ducking in and out of the darkening clouds above. Someone, probably the local teenagers, had built a wall of rocks around the plunge pool, no doubt to deepen the water and make it more interesting to swim in. It was an inviting prospect.

Mikal set up his tripod on a slope next to the rocky wall of the gorge and we sat down and waited for the sun to reappear. Overhead a thick layer of caprock reached out almost 20 feet into nothing. I sat there wondering how long it had been that way — 100 years? Or 500? At what moment on what day in eternity would it chose to come crashing down? I know I'm always thinking about such things. It's not so much fear as the curiosity of the fatalist. Once, when we were camping north of Kingston, a huge tree, at least 100 years old, gave up the ghost and fell over into a lake not 15 seconds after we had passed under it. We could see that it was rotten at the core but, other than mere coincidence, what had caused it to keel over at that instant? Anyway, if the overhang had chosen this day to fall, we would have a good deal less than 15 seconds to scramble for our lives.

As we packed up to leave, we discovered that someone had leaned an old piece of iron ladder against the side of the gorge just behind us. It got us up to a series of ledges by which we quickly regained the crest of the falls.

Inglis Falls

On the Sydenham River

Height – 18 m (58.5 ft)   Crest Width – 6 m (19.5 ft)   N 44:31:53 W 80:56:10

Inglis Falls Conservation Area

Best Time to View: All year round. A substantial millpond above the falls ensures the water supply except in the driest of summers. It faces north and is wide open to the sky. It's unquestionably a cascade.

Responsible Authority: Grey Sauble Conservation Authority, (519) 376-3076

How to Get There: Go north on Highway 10 to Rockford, which is just south of Owen Sound. Turn left on County Road 18. Go west to Inglis Falls Road. Turn right. The entrance to the conservation area is just a short distance on your right. It's a popular spot but the facilities are well laid out and there's plenty of parking.

No waterfall on the Escarpment is more cherished than this one. Its lovely countenance smiles at you from the pages of every tourist brochure. All over town, signs point you in its direction. People go out of their way to ask if you've seen Inglis Falls.

To say that it is 18 meters high or that it's a cascade doesn't begin to tell you what this falls is really like. Photographs reveal something of its character but they don't convey its size. Only when you are able to stand there and see it for yourself can you appreciate how truly exceptional this waterfall is. The Escarpment appears to have opened up and spilled forth enormous blocks of stone and tons of water into the gorge below. That's the first surprise. The second comes as you study it more closely and realize that it is not one waterfall but many little ones, each falling one into the other, all the way to the bottom.

From its narrow crest the falls flares out like a skirt. It must be close to 100 meters wide at the bottom. Indeed, when there's a great deal of water flowing, it resembles not so much a skirt as a lacy crinoline.

A hundred and fifty years ago, when Owen Sound was still Sydenham Bay and the journey overland from Toronto meant trekking for days through dark, entangled forest, some people were already going out of their way to see Inglis Falls. In 1851, Lord Elgin, the governor general, took the long but easy way around, through the lakes, and arrived by steamer.

In 1874 another governor general, the Earl of Dufferin, made the same journey. It was a very dry year and far less than the usual 13,000,000 gallons a day was cascading over the falls. The local people, fearing he would not be suitably impressed, temporarily dammed the river to build up the volume. When the vice-regal party was in sight they let it go and for a while the falls took on the

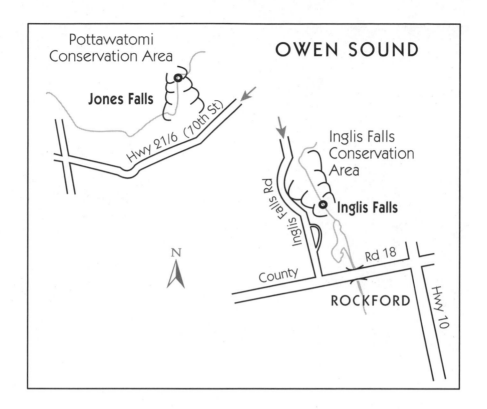

fulsomeness of spring runoff. (It took a lot to impress Lord Dufferin. He once said he was at his best in the morning, tapping his egg.)

There have been times when a surfeit of water turned Inglis into a fearsome thing, when for all its breadth and openness it couldn't handle the volume of water forced upon it by the swollen Sydenham River. The last time that happened was in 1977, when so much water came down at one time that a great portion of it flowed around the falls and created a new but temporary waterfall on the high wall of the gorge to the east.

Owen Sound and its hinterland began to develop in the middle of the 19th century, at a time that coincided with one of the most dramatic periods of immigration in Canadian history. Every year tens of thousands of people came to Canada, many of them fleeing starvation in Ireland or driven from their humble homes in the Scottish Highlands by greed-ridden landowners. For most of them it must have truly been the best of times and the worst of times. They fled death and deprivation by sailing away to the promised land of Canada but they often brought with them cholera, typhus, diphtheria and smallpox.

If they survived the voyage and the diseases that dogged them, they came ashore some of the most determined men and women this country has ever had

Owen Sound's Inglis Falls in 1862 during construction of the great mill.
COUNTY OF GREY-OWEN SOUND MUSEUM

the good fortune to receive. Often the history books, or the textbooks at least, have made them out to be dour, even bovine in nature. Their letters and journals suggest they were capable of being anything but:

> I long to crack a night or two with you. … to think of persons like us, inured to the sweets and luxuries of London, launched out to Canada to raw pork and Yankified rum and a soft bed of leaves beneath the wild wood tree.
> An excerpt from "In the Days of the Canada Company" (1896)

There's nothing of the hayseed in the man who wrote that letter.

And Peter Inglis and Anne Carroll were not hayseeds either. He was a young millwright from St. Andrews in Fife who came to the New World on his own, in 1843. She came from Ireland with her sister and widowed mother. Peter and Anne met, married and raised seven children. They gave their name to the falls and eventually became quite well off.

Somehow the young Peter found the wherewithal to buy the existing gristmill and sawmill at what was then Sydenham Falls, along with 300 surrounding acres. What is more, he knew what to do with this valuable property once he had it in hand. Everyone who had tried to make a go of it at the falls had failed. He thrived. In a few years he had a handful of mills operating and he was attracting farmers from as far away as Collingwood, Mount Forest and Paisley. For several years it was the biggest industry in Owen Sound. And for 90 years it was the only business the men of the Inglis family knew.

In 1862, Peter Inglis built a new gristmill, one that was the envy of the Bruce Peninsula. It was a great towering wooden structure that rose from the water halfway down the falls. The mill outlasted him by a good many years. He died in 1901. It burned in 1945. Few of the old mills were able to escape the inevitability of fire that long. There's not a trace of it left, but you can get a very romantic impression of what it looked like from the mural by artist Allen C. Hilgendorf on the wall of the remaining stable building.

Peter Inglis also had a woolen mill where farmers could bring the shearings from their flocks to be cleaned and carded. They gave him one third of the wool for doing this dirty job and took the rest home to turn into the famous homespun of pioneer times. Homespun was dreary gray in color — quite on purpose. Interestingly, it wasn't a dye that gave it that shade but a mix of fibers from black and white sheep. In an age when keeping the family's clothes clean was one of the most laborious tasks on a list of many, white was not a practical choice. They did add a dash of color now and then, using common plants for the source. Dandelion roots produced red. Onion skin gave fabric an earthy tone.

In the early years, cash crops were small and transportation was difficult. Most farm families brought what they could to the mills at Inglis Falls on ox carts. Some actually carried their grain or wool on their backs. Frequently they stayed for a few days, sleeping on the ground near the falls. It was a busy but relaxing place and it was as close to a vacation as many of them would ever come. Some stayed longer than planned and ran out of food. No one thought that a crisis. They could always scrape up enough wheat kernels from the floor of the mill to make a pancake or a scone.

It's still a place families are reluctant to leave. Stand at the wall next to the crest of the falls on a hot, bright summer day and you can see them on the rocks below, some picnicking, others sunbathing, still others soaking in the cool pools of swirling water. Raise your eyes to the gorge beyond and you can see a long way to the north. There's nothing but forest, clear to the horizon. Beyond Inglis Falls Conservation Area is Harrison Park, a large, heavily forested tract that straddles the Sydenham River all the way to the center of town. It's quite a prize for a small, proud city to have in its midst.

Jones Falls

On the Pottawatomi River

Height – 12 m (39 ft)   Crest Width – 10 m (32.5ft)   N 44:33:55 W 80:59:11

Pottawatomi Conservation Area

Best Time to View: All year round. Water levels will be down in the summer months, but Jones is a waterfall like Webster's; though its character changes with the diminished flow, it's no less attractive. It faces south and is open to the sky. This is a steep cascade with a wide but inaccessible ledge about a third of the way down.

Responsible Authority: Grey Sauble Conservation Authority, (519) 376-3076

How to Get There: Take Highways 21 and 6 (10th Street) east from the center of Owen Sound. In minutes you'll find yourself making a long, gentle climb up the Escarpment. Look for a large, darkly painted barn on your left. When you see it, pull over and look to your right. You'll find yourself looking straight at Jones Falls, about 100 meters away. You can access it from this point; the Bruce Trail passes close by and crosses the river just below the falls. Resist the temptation. No one wants you to park there anyway. Continue driving instead to the top of the Escarpment, to where Highway 6 branches off and goes north. Turn right and pull into the headquarters of the Grey Bruce Tourism Association. You'll find the path to the falls at the back of the parking lot.

The tourist literature had us hyped for a spectacular walk, one that might even be a bit dangerous in spots, so we were a little disappointed when at first all we encountered was flat land and scrub bush. Not that the going wasn't dangerous, but only because it had rained hard the previous afternoon and the many rounded stones underfoot were precariously slippery.

The trail didn't begin to live up to the hype till we reached the banks of the Pottawatomi a few minutes later. It's a stream of some breadth but extremely shallow, and it was running hard over a long series of rocky ledges on its way to the falls. In the cool morning light the water looked pristine and temptingly potable.

As we made our way east the sun came smiling through the trees, warming the dark waters as they passed under a footbridge, just meters before plunging over the brink. Everything in the woods ahead of us sparkled with yesterday's raindrops. We found we could safely walk out into the sunlight at the very edge of the falls, and even do it with dry feet. On one side the rushing water was framed by a wall of dolostone that was beautifully overhung by lazy white cedars. Pale green ferns, just enough of them to give the scene a final artistic touch, sat demurely in the crevasses between the rocks. I thought how wonderfully Japanese it looked. Then I

Even in the midst of a summer drought, Jones Falls is a beauty.

stopped myself. Japanese? The landscape I was looking at was as Canadian as anything I've ever seen. There are ten thousand little spots like this, each with that
same aesthetic mix of water, stone, cedar and fern, each with that same austere
look of purity that marks it as typically Canadian.

   We discovered to our delight that we could climb much higher, to a point well
above the falls. From here the water appeared to be gushing right out of the forest
That did look unCanadian. It looked downright tropical in fact.

   A man and his young son soon joined us. He spent some minutes exhorting
the boy to admire the falls, hoping he could somehow coax him into being
enthralled. "Look! Look at it!" he commanded. "Doesn't it look great!" As every
parent knows, or should know, the biggest turnoff for a child is to have an adult
insist that they appreciate something. However, knowing it and stopping yourself
from doing it are two different things. In any case, the boy was more interested in
climbing up and down the surrounding rocks, and that set his father off on a new
round of exhortations: "Don't! How many times am I going to tell you? Now get
down from there!" And then, as suddenly as they had appeared, the exasperated
father and the self-absorbed little boy were gone and we had Jones Falls and the
lovely Sunday morning to ourselves again.

We climbed back down to the footbridge and crossed to the other side. Here we saw that the morning sun, striking the water at the lower edge of the falls, was giving it the texture of liquid glass. It had the potential to be a great photograph, though Mikal was quick to tell me it would be tricky and would take some careful doing to pull it off. The pool at the bottom of the falls was in sunlight; the water at the ledge was backlit; and the rocks and trees in the foreground were in deep shadow. That's head-scratching time for any serious photographer.

While he dug deep into his equipment bag for his faithful spot meter, I offered as many unwanted suggestions as I thought he might be able to handle and then drifted off by myself. You can't take great photographs by committee, no matter how closely the members of the committee are related.

Each new waterfall seemed to bring us into the presence of increasingly interesting collections of rocks. Here at Jones Falls they were inexpressibly odd and wonderful. One set of big, perfectly round boulders, standing just feet from the crest of the falls, looked as if they had been designed by some ultra-progressive architect for a vastly upscale and expensive playground. In fact, if you saw them in a playground, you'd dismiss them for looking artificial and contrived. Yet here they existed, as real as rocks can be.

Other rocks, including some that were quite large, had been sliced in half so neatly you'd swear someone had cut them on a bandsaw. No doubt the frost did that. Still others looked so gnarled and anguished it was impossible to imagine what horrors they'd been through.

The first people to settle on the Escarpment, on what was originally called the Niagara Ridge, were convinced that its rocky outcroppings were the result of some sort of volcanic activity. We now know the true explanation to be much more complex, much more compelling than that. Still, you don't have to know or even care about knowing to have some affection for stone, as many an architect, stonemason, sculptor or antiquarian will tell you. There's something about the cool, intimate feel of it, its ageless dignity. In a world that won't stop changing — can't stop changing! — stone is that rare thing that remains unmoved and certain.

When I finally wandered back to see how Mikal was doing, I found him winding a roll of film back through the camera, confident that the picture he had been hoping for was safely on film. I looked at my watch. We had spent nearly three hours at Jones Falls, three absorbing hours, and not once had we allowed time to rush us along. Time doesn't fly when you're having fun; it ceases to exist.

Indian Falls

On Indian Creek

Height – 15 m (49 ft)   Crest Width – 12 m (39 ft)   N 44:37:24   W 80:57:00

Indian Falls Conservation Area

Best Time to View: As summer progresses and the creek dries up, Indian Falls changes from a curtain to a ribbon falls and loses some of its charm. It faces east and is open to the sky.

Responsible Authority: Grey Sauble Conservation Authority, (519) 376-3076

How to Get There: Take the Eddie Sargent Parkway (2nd Avenue West) north from the center of Owen Sound. This will take you up the west shore of the bay. In five minutes you'll come to Balmy Beach. Keep an eye open for the sign indicating the entrance to Indian Falls Conservation Area, on the left. There's plenty of parking.

We thought for an instant we had come to the wrong place. The parking lot was full of pickups and 4 X 4s and a rowdy crowd was hooting and hollering over a baseball game being played in the field to the north. It looked like fun but it seemed out of place in the quiet of a conservation area.

We knew that somewhere along the back of the open area, probably under a big oak or maple, we'd find the trail to the falls. It always seemed to be that way and this time was no different.

Minutes later the sounds from the ball diamond faded and disappeared from our presence, drowned out by the rushing waters of Indian Creek. The hike was a lot like the one we had taken along the Pottawatomi, the same clear, glittering water, the same swift-flowing stream, the same "cobblestone" path along its banks, the same forest of shadowy cedars, only this time it was evening, not morning, and we were heading upstream, not down.

About halfway to the falls the path rose sharply. It was so steep near the top of the rise that we finished the climb on step logs. Now we were on level ground again, high above the creek, passing through a grove of young beech trees. Already people had given in to the urge to carve love vows in their slim trunks. It made me think of the big beech tree we had seen on the way to Anthea's Falls, the one that had "1947" inscribed so prominently in its trunk. Would people passing here in the middle of the 21st century, seeing 1999 carved on one of these trees, be curious about us? Would they wonder what thoughts were in our heads as we contemplated the unknowns of the new century, a century already half over for them?

As usual we could hear the falls before we could see it. It sounded like it had a good bit of water in it. It was the sound of it no doubt that prompted the Nawash people to call it Drum Falls.

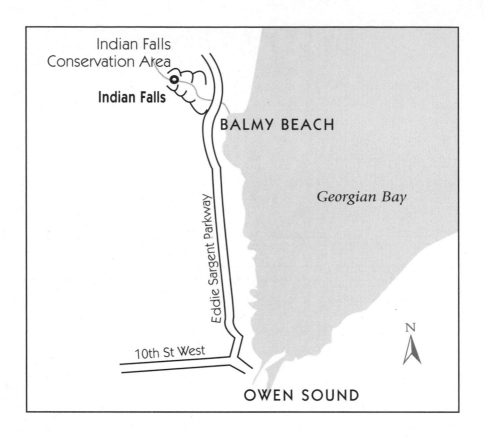

When we finally sighted it, at that time of day, in that light, it took our breath away. There was indeed a good bit of water in it, long, lazy curtains of it descending into the darkening gorge below. You could easily have walked behind that transparent wall of water without getting wet — if the shale below the overhanging caprock hadn't been so loose and unstable looking. The water had undermined the falls a dozen feet or more.

A few feet from the edge of the falls there was a considerable overhang that had cracked and pulled away from the face of the cliff. It leaned precariously over the gorge. Looking at it, I thought all it would take from me would be one good shove and it would go crashing into the water below. It's crazy notions like that, no doubt, that prompted the Conservation Authority to put up the fence that stood between me and that swooning bit of rock. Down in the gorge we could see another huge piece that had fallen. It had split into layers that were so neatly stacked they looked like giant slices of bread that had fallen from the end of a loaf.

Above the falls Indian Creek was as broad and as still as a millpond, a polished mirror held up to the sky to reflect the sultry pinks and orangey yellows in the great clouds scudding overhead. It was a scene that Constable might have painted, and probably would have if he could have seen it as we were seeing it. I

Quiet waters at the crest of Owen Sound's Indian Falls.

say that because beyond the creek, beyond the big stones that kept the bulrushes from encroaching on the water's edge, there was not the usual cedar forest but a meadow, a meadow in which rolls of new-mowed hay had been left to dry, in which a lone oak towered majestically, and in which there was, believe it or not, a flock of sheep grazing in the rich evening light. Nature imitating Constable…

If this scene could somehow have been transported to the English Lake District, it would be world famous. If it existed in the Shenandoah Valley of Virginia or the Loire Valley of France, it would be world famous. But it was here, in Ontario, and only the people of Owen Sound and a few of the rest of us knew about it or cared about it. I was of two minds about that. It's nice to have people come from far and wide to admire the things you treasure but it was nice, too, to be sharing this peerless waterfall on this priceless evening with nobody else but a family of farmers from the Ontario hinterland.

We stood there a long while, watching the light slowly fade, watching the family's two girls — young women, really — take off their shoes to kick and splash in the water and squeal like children. They were just feet from the edge of the falls and the long drop to the rocks below. Curious how people will do things like that without concern, even people who otherwise might be afraid to go to the edge and look down.

As we watched, a cormorant flew over our heads, clearing the crest of the falls by 10 or 15 feet. It was hard for me to make out his markings in that light, but Mikal said it was a doubled-crested cormorant. Moments later a kingfisher went shooting by us in the opposite direction. Both birds were obviously heading for some favored roost for the night. It was time for us to do the same.

The Escarpment Hither and Yon

The Niagara Escarpment stretches far beyond the borders of Ontario. That's a surprise to those of us who grew up thinking it was something uniquely our own.

Its presence can be detected as far east as the foothills of the Appalachians. It makes its first appearance above ground near Rochester, New York, where people often referred to it as the Onandaga Scarp. Between Rochester and Lewiston, where it crosses into Ontario, there's a string of waterfalls. No one is more familiar with them than Scott Ensminger of North Tonawanda, New York. He's become the ultimate waterfall "collector" with his Western New York Waterfall Survey (http://www.geocities.com/Yosemite/Rapids/8910/index.html). As of January 1, 2,000, his waterfall count was an astounding 712! Believe it or not, Buffalo's Erie County topped the list with 125 waterfalls.

To the north, the Escarpment dips below the waters of Lake Huron at Tobermory to reemerge as Manitoulin and Cockburn Islands. The Escarpment is the primary reason for the existence of those islands and the only reason Georgian Bay is separated so definitively from Lake Huron.

There are several lovely small waterfalls on Manitoulin, including the exquisite Bridal Veil Falls, which has been pictured in so many brochures it's virtually the island's trademark.

The Escarpment continues westward through Upper Michigan, running close to the Lake Michigan shore but actually facing north, toward Lake Superior.

Michigan is rich in waterfalls and fortunate in the number of enthusiastic people who have taken a serious interest in them. Bill and Ruth Penrose. for example, began collecting waterfalls as a hobby. It soon became an obsession. They were the first to go looking for and find every waterfall in the state. They published their findings in a book, *A Guide to 199 Michigan Waterfalls*. (Friede Publications, Davidson, MI)

Bob Reszka of the Michigan Department of Natural Resources shows off his waterfall collection in public slide shows. He puts the total number of falls in the state at 133, all but one of them in the Upper Peninsula. (The discrepancy in numbers between Mr. Reszka and the Penroses arises from differing definitions. There's a quite gray area between what some see as a steep rapid and others as a gentle cascade.) When we asked Dr. Reszka how many of Michigan's waterfalls are on the Escarpment or the Niagaran Reef, as it's known in the Great Lakes State, he got out his maps and did a search for us. The result surprised both him and us. None! The major reason for this is that the streams all flow away from the Escarpment, south into Lake Michigan.

The Escarpment continues well beyond Michigan, turning southward in the western part of the state to form the Garden Peninsula, then disappearing beneath the waters of Lake Michigan to reappear in Wisconsin as the Door Peninsula. The two peninsulas enclose the body of water everyone knows as Green Bay. Dr. Don Mikulie of the Illinois Geological Survey is yet another scientist with a particular interest in waterfalls. He says there are at least half a dozen fine small ones on the Door Peninsula. All face west, for here again the Escarpment has its back to Lake Michigan.

The Escarpment peters out north of Milwaukee, though evidence of it can be found as far south as Indiana.

The ice age had more to do with the look of the landscape in the Great Lakes area than any other event in geological history. For a start, the weight of the glaciers was incredible. They were often 2 or 3 kilometers thick, perhaps as much as 4 kilometers in the case of the Laurentide Ice Sheet. This depressed the land considerably. And because the ice moved and shifted as the glaciers increased or decreased in size, it gouged and scoured the surface, wearing away many geographic features. It planed off parts of the Escarpment so thoroughly in some places it's no longer visible. That, incidentally, is another reason there are no waterfalls on the Niagaran Reef in Upper Michigan; there isn't much of it left there for them to flow over.

Geologists calculate that at one time the Escarpment was as much as 200 kilometers to the east, which would put it about midway between Toronto and Ottawa. Over millions of years it has eroded that much and that far! On the other hand, its cliffs and headlands are probably higher now than they have been for thousands of years. That's because the land is still rising after being relieved of the weight of the ice.

The glaciers were responsible for much of the way the Escarpment looks today but they didn't create it. The ice age lasted a million years. The rocks that makes up the Escarpment were formed 350 to 420 million years before that. If you stop to study the strata exposed by the waterfalls and you let your eye run from the top layer of hard dolostone down to the crumbly red Queenston shale at the bottom, you captured in a single glance about 20 to 25 million years of history from the Ordovician and Silurian periods. At one time the Escarpment was called the Silurian Scarp.

If you look at a map of the Great Lakes and follow the line of the Escarpment from Rochester to Milwaukee, you will see that it is almost circular in shape. What it is, in reality, is the exposed rim of a much larger geological feature known as the Michigan Basin, which is centered in that state's Lower Peninsula. There's even a professional organization called the Michigan Basin Society. (Wouldn't it make for interesting conversation to have that on your calling card.)

The Michigan Basin is what remains today of the shallow, tropical sea that existed 400 to 425 million years ago. The caprock of the Escarpment is the hardened, fossilized sediment from the bottom of that sea. It's what is known as biogenic rock because it's made up in large part of shells, skeletons and corals, most of them from the middle of the Silurian period. These, in a very real sense, have been cemented together. (The first Portland cement produced in Canada

In late April there's still ice at the bottom of Hilton Falls.

came from a section of the Escarpment near Indian Falls.) It's because of this that the Escarpment is one of the richest areas in the world for fossils from the Paleozoic era, especially in the upper reaches around Collingwood.

The Escarpment, or at least that part of it that's in Ontario, has been designated a World Biosphere Reserve by UNESCO. That puts it in the company of other unique places such as the Galapagos Islands, the Serengeti Plain and the Florida Everglades.

The biosphere is the envelope of gases that surrounds the Earth and retains heat and sustains life. A Biosphere Reserve is about sustaining life. It's recognition that there is a significant ecological feature in our midst and that we need to handle it with care and forethought — and strike a balance between preservation and development. The goal, ultimately, is to maintain the integrity of the Escarpment, to ensure that its existence as a single entity is not lost through piecemeal development and exploitation of its resources.

The Niagara Escarpment is the longest continuous forest area in Southern Ontario. Its streams, ponds and marshes support 91 species of fish. Its woodlands, bluffs and meadows support 325 species of birds, 1,545 species of plants, 288 species of moss. There are 39 species of reptiles and amphibians, including the shy Massasauga rattlesnake, which is found only in the quieter upper reaches. There are 47 species of mammals, including the elusive wildcat, whose presence in the Bruce

Classic view of Hogg's Falls.

Peninsula was confirmed only after the Ministry of Natural Resources had DNA tests done on suspected stool samples.

We have searched for but haven't yet found tiny Battlefield Falls on Stoney Creek, and Sue Powell of the Niagara Escarpment Commission tells us we missed another falls on Silver Creek to the northwest of Georgetown. We did go looking for it one afternoon but obviously looked in the wrong place.

The more you learn about the Niagara Escarpment the more fascinating it becomes. That's why this chapter is at the end of the book rather the beginning, where you might expect to find it. We hoped to whet your appetite first with the excitement and fascination of discovering the waterfalls.

We have been able to show the way, we think, to most of the accessible waterfalls in the Southern Ontario portion of the Escarpment — 38 of them, including 32 of substantial size and volume. Many of the remaining 20 or 30 are on private property, though not all of them. Just as this was being written Ron Yorke, Trail Director of the Dufferin Hi-Land Club of the Bruce Trail Association, e-mailed us about a small waterfall he had discovered to the east of Noisy River Provincial Park. He even sent us a picture of it. We'll have to wait till summer to go looking for it and hundreds more elsewhere. Chuck Grant, Trail Director of the Beaver Valley Club, told us about three more, though all it seems are on private property.

The lacy loveliness of Ancaster's Tiffany Falls.

As noted in the introduction, we were convinced there were no waterfalls north of Indian Falls because the streams in the Bruce Peninsula all flow away from the Escarpment. Then we heard from Walter Brewer, a member of the Toronto Club of the Bruce Trail Association. He sent us a picture of a small falls he had discovered near Devil's Monument on Dyer's Bay. There's no stream there to feed it but water seeping underground from nearby Britain Lake has emerged from under the caprock to produce the waterfall. John Riley of the Nature Conservancy of Canada confirmed Mr. Brewer's observations and told us he knew of a similar waterfall further north on Dyer's Bay.

It's obvious that you won't run out of waterfalls to "collect" after you've gone looking for and found the ones chronicled in this guide. There are more to be found on the Escarpment and hundreds elsewhere.

Perhaps one day there will be people and organizations interested enough to start a Great Lakes waterfall survey. As you've just read, most of the work has already been done in New York and Michigan. The Ohio Department of Natural Resources had a waterfall survey operating as far back as the early '80s. But little seems to have been done in Ontario. No one knows how many waterfalls there are in those parts of the province drained by the lakes, though every falls is obviously known to someone. Finding them and documenting their locations and their history and compiling a comprehensive list could be great fun for a lot of people. The idea is there for the taking.

Having finished this guidebook, we now have time to work on a website. Look for www.collectingwaterfalls.ca in the fall of 2000. Click on and tell us about your own waterfall discoveries and experiences.

Photographing Waterfalls

As photographic subjects, waterfalls and rapids are unique. You can take pictures of them all day long and always catch them at the peak of the action. There are two things, however, that one needs to pay particular attention to: shutter speed and the way the light plays on the subject.

By altering shutter speed you can give a range of different looks to a waterfall. At 1/125 of a second or faster, under average lighting conditions, you can stop the action dead, so much so that you may lose the feeling of flow. At 1/15 to 1/8, there'll be enough movement in the picture to imply action. At 1/4 or slower the water will take on a milky, sentimental look much favored by some for posters and calendars.

Most of the pictures in this book were shot at 1/15 or 1/8 of a second. There are times, however, when other settings will give you the picture you want. Faster shutter speeds are useful when you're working in close to a falls, trying to capture detail or composing an abstract. Then you may want the instant of exposure to be quick enough to freeze the water droplets in midair. The slower speeds are best

A photographer in midstream aims his camera at Webster's Falls.

A slow shutter gives Hilton Falls a rich, milky look.

when there's very little water in a falls or rapid and you want to make it stand out from the surrounding landscape. You might also want to slow the shutter if, for example, you're concentrating on the water at the point it enters the plunge pool. The falling water will look milky but the ripples in the pool will have a lovely sense of movement to them.

If there's any one factor that separates great photographs from all the others, it's the way the photographer uses the lighting. You can turn almost any light condition to your advantage, if you stop and study its potential for making your picture something special rather than something likely to end up in the reject box.

Sunlight is always richer and more dramatic early or late in the day. With your own eyes you can see that it has more pink in it in the morning, more yellow as evening approaches. The light of spring is crisper, clearer. The light of autumn is warmer with a touch of haze in it. Wonderful photographs, however, aren't always shot on wonderful days. Overcast, rainy, snowy, even foggy days can turn a waterfall into a moody, dramatic thing. The trick then is to keep the sky out of the picture or at least keep if from blending into the waterfall. An overcast sky registers a deadly white on film. That, all by itself, has killed many a picture.

Bright sunny days, especially summer days, can be as challenging as any. Water compounds the brightness and the contrast with the shadowy areas around a waterfall is often too great for ordinary shooting. You can employ a polarizer to lessen the glare from the water. Nevertheless, you may find yourself looking for vantage points from which you can frame out much of the surrounding darkness.

It is when the obvious shot looks unpromising and you start looking for alternatives that you become most creative. Then you find yourself carefully studying reflections in the pool at the base of a falls or in the smooth water at the brink. Surprisingly, reflections can be found in fast-moving water, too. You may discover unusual colors or shapes in stretches of water you would otherwise frame out of the picture. Many a great photograph owes its appeal to the reflection of the sky or clouds or surrounding trees, bushes, rocks or flowers. In winter it can be the ice formations that are part of every waterfall, especially when you have sunlight to play with.

You can usually see more of a waterfall, from more angles, when the trees are bare. One of the best times for shooting, though it's very short, only a few days, is when the buds have burst and there's green in the trees but the leaves are not big enough yet to obstruct your view.

If you experience a lot of sun sparkle, use a star filter, if you have one. If not, use the polarizer to get the best from this always-brilliant effect. Some photographers will breathe on the lens just before they snap a picture, to give it a misty look. There's a line that separates reality from hokeyness. It's your choice whether you chose to cross it or not.

Blue skies are beautiful but sometimes it's difficult to bring them into a picture and make them work with brightly sunlit water. It's easier if you can frame a bit of rock between the sky and the water.

Waterfalls produce rainbows. You can enhance their color by using a polarizer and rotating it until you achieve maximum intensity. Watch carefully through the lens as you do this, however. If you turn it too far, you'll lose the rainbow entirely.

If you're shooting in midsummer and drought has reduced the flow of water, as it so often does, don't go home without pictures. Use your telephoto or portrait lens to get in close. There are a lot of fine pictures to be found by searching a waterfall for interesting detail, especially in those areas where the sun plays on the water.

Where do you point your meter to get an accurate reading? If the waterfall takes up most of the frame, look for a gray rock somewhere in its midst and read the light from that. Then stop down half a stop more to ensure that you get detail in the water.

If the scene is deeply shadowed, use a warming filter to take away the bluish tint you'll get otherwise. But stop and think about the consequences before you do. If the water is white and the surrounding rocks are gray and there's nothing else of color in the picture, the warming filter will transform it into something close to a black-and-white photo, and probably a very ordinary one at that. The bluish tint could make the difference between a throwaway and a keeper.

If low light levels make it impossible to shoot at the desired shutter speed on 100 ASA, you might think about going to a faster film. You'll get somewhat more grain but unless you're planning to enlarge your pictures to coffee-table-book size, you can probably live with it. If you do switch, you may also want to switch to color negative, if you've been shooting transparencies. Negative will give you slightly better quality at the higher ASA ratings.

If you've got your eye on publishing your pictures, you should know that most publishers prefer transparencies. Some will accept nothing but. Transparencies, by the way, are best at bringing out the highlights of a scene. Print film is better at producing detail in the shadow areas.

Under the heading Best Time to View, we have indicated the direction each waterfall faces and whether or not it's affected by forest cover. It may be helpful to know such things when you're trying to decide which waterfalls to visit and when.

A tripod is essential. The shutter speeds are too slow for hand-held work. Keep a pair of rubber boots in the trunk of your car; there will always be that perfect shot that you can't get to unless you go splashing out into the middle of the stream. A pair of light plastic rainpants is also a good accessory. Then you won't think twice about where you kneel.

There are two photographer's tricks that are worth knowing, if you don't already. The first is called bracketing. Use it when you've set up a shot that you really like but the light values are complex and you're not confident of the reading you're getting from your meter. Take one shot using the setting indicated by the meter. Take a second shot that is one stop less than the first. Take a third that is one stop more. One of the three will turn out to be the picture you're hoping for. Bracketing compensates for subtle light values your meter may not be able to pick up.

The second trick is one you use when framing a shot. As you look through the viewfinder, mentally divide the picture into three equal parts horizontally and

Spectacular Webster's Falls in midwinter.

Photographing Waterfalls

then three equal parts vertically. Now make sure that anything you want to feature as the center of interest is positioned where two of these imaginary lines intersect. What this does is keep you from putting the object that is the center of interest right smack in the middle of the frame, where it will invariably result in something that looks a lot like a snapshot. It's a particularly helpful trick if you're planning to pose someone in front of a waterfall.

And if you do include people in your waterfall pictures, try to capture them in poses that are natural. Think of them as portraits, not snapshots. Have them stand with their shoulders at an angle to the camera. Have them look a little to one side, at something beyond the lens. Shoot looking up at them or down on them. If they insist on mugging for the camera and giving you the expected "cheesy" grin, there's an old newspaper photographer's trick that works every time. Pretend you've taken the shot. Say "Great, that's it!" then trip the shutter as everybody relaxes. For some reason, people chose that moment to laugh and smile in the most natural way.

The best waterfall photos give the viewer a feeling for the place. It's a hard thing to convey if you yourself don't have a feel for it. Explore every vantage point. Shoot the falls from as many angles as you can. This will force you to look at it differently, to get a sense of its character and mood. Pretend you're a professional on assignment and your reputation is on the line. Refuse to leave until you've got a whole roll of pictures good enough to make the cover of a magazine. Creating a little intensity for yourself is not only fun but you'll be surprised by how many truly good pictures it will produce.

If you have interesting rocks or water in the foreground but they're darkened by shadow, try using your flash as a fill light. Remove it from the camera, however, and hold it away from you to avoid a flat look. Much of the flash will no doubt be lost in the daylight but often it's just enough to make the picture.

For an unusual view of a waterfall, try getting right down at shoe-top level. That will shift the emphasis to the foreground and to the plunge pool or the downstream rapids. Don't, however, split the composition half and half between the foreground and the falls. Give one or the other about two-thirds of the picture. For an example, see the photo of DeCew Falls on page 49.

Finally, if you have a camcorder, why not shoot a relaxation video or a tape to play back during quiet conversation — especially during the dead of winter when memories of summer are most appreciated. You have to use a tripod for it to be an effective mood-maker because every shot needs to be several minutes long. Walk away from the camera once you start a shot, sit down, take it easy, but don't talk! That will ruin the mood. Record a total of at least 30 minutes, longer if you can. Later you may want to add music but watch it through a couple of times before you do. The sound of the falling water, even more than the picture, will be the key to the mood you want to create. Don't let anything but the most deeply felt music distract you from it.